The Legacy of *Atlanta*

A SHORT HISTORY

Webb Garrison

PEACHTREE PUBLISHERS, LTD.

Published by
PEACHTREE PUBLISHERS, LTD.
494 Armour Circle, N.E.
Atlanta, Georgia 30324

Manufactured in the United States of America

2nd Printing (1992)

Design by Merry Leigh Giarratano

Library of Congress Catalog Card Number 86-63531

ISBN 0-934601-14-3

CONTENTS

The Legacy of *Atlanta*

From Standing Peachtree To Spaghetti Junction: An Overview

Tustunugee Hutkee led his hand-picked braves northward. White men who knew him as William McIntosh had already rewarded him richly for his role in negotiating treaties with his own people, the Creeks. Preparing to meet with Cherokees in the fall of 1823, he hoped to bribe chieftains to cede their lands.

Coweta Town was the major center of Lower Creek power. Big Cherokee villages were located at Etowah and Allatoona and Nacoochee. To travel between them, it was necessary to cross the turbulent Chattahoochee. That meant heavy use of the shallow ford at present-day Roswell.

Warriors and traders habitually used the shallow ford in going between today's Columbus, Georgia, and Chattanooga, Tennessee. Their all-important north-south trail was crossed by east-west trails a few miles west of gigantic Rock Mountain. Early white explorers came to know the site, and the surrounding village, as Standing Peachtree.

Peach trees were not native to the region. Hence, that prominent landmark may have been a huge *pitch* tree, or resin-yielding pine. Whether pure or corrupted, the tree's name has attached to more than a score of Atlanta streets, plus countless business establishments.

Tustunugee's 1823 journey to meet with Cherokees was futile. Two years later, though, he persuaded the Lower Creeks to cede all their Georgia lands. His first cousin, Georgia Governor George McIntosh Troup, had earlier sworn to drive out the Cherokees. When these aboriginals took to the Trail of Tears in 1838, opposition to westward and northern expansion by the white man ended.

Standing Peachtree, plus vast surrounding regions, was firmly in the grasp of settlers.

Not that whites of an earlier era had considered the place to be of importance. Far from the coast and not located on a navigable river, it was no site for a thriving town. Even the roughly built stockade erected in 1814 and often called Fort Peachtree was, at best, a tiny frontier outpost.

Early enchantment with canals as the means to develop north-central Georgia had faded. Legislators turned to newfangled transportation by steam and chartered three railroads. One of them, the state-owned Western & Atlantic, was designed to run from Chattanooga to a spot not far east of the Chattahoochee River.

Veteran military engineer Stephen H. Long was selected to survey the route and build the line. From the start, it was expected to be linked with others from Augusta, Columbus and Macon. For the river crossing, Long selected a spot close to Standing Peachtree.   Roswell

Topography dictated his choice of a terminus for the line. A ridge with a grade of just 285 feet in eight miles, running from the river, was the ideal spot. Some time in September, 1837, Long or his aide, Albert Brisbane, drove the stake that marked the terminus of the planned railroad — and the beginning of Atlanta.

Within a decade, the railroad village had become a transportation hub at which three major lines met. By 1857 the fast-growing center was being called "The Gate City" because of its role as a rail center.

Much of the freight pulled by locomotives rolled through and past Atlanta. Some passengers got off and became permanent residents. By 1860 the once-remote site had a bank, a newspaper, and nearly ten thousand residents.

Atlantans made a bid for their town to become the capital of the Confederate States of America but lost out to older and much bigger Richmond, Virginia. However, converging railroads made it a key supply center with no counterpart in any rebel state.

Small wonder that Ulysses S. Grant and William T. Sherman recognized that the little city must be captured, at any cost. Pounded for weeks by Federal artillery, it was surrendered late in 1864 by a civilian — Mayor James M. Burned

Tustunugee Hutkee, or William McIntosh

Calhoun. Most of Atlanta was burned and most citizens fled or were forced to leave.

Early 1865 saw the rail center transformed into a U.S. military post. Many analysts would have said that it would never recover from wounds of war.

Atlantans, whether by birth or by adoption, largely ignored the impossibility of making a comeback. New and better buildings replaced those left in ruins when the March to the Sea began. Additional rail lines reached the little city. Ambitious plans for higher education of blacks led to establishment of Atlanta University.

Less than a decade after being nearly demolished, Atlanta had rebuilt and had replaced Milledgeville as capital of the state. Business and professional leaders — many of them born and reared in the North — guided and prodded for more and better colleges, newspapers, hotels and parks.

Just a quarter century after war's end, the population had jumped to sixty-five thousand; by 1900 it was just under ninety thousand. Arrival of the Seaboard Air Line Railroad in 1892 solidified the city's position as a key transportation center.

Fort Peachtree, as recreated in 1976

In the city that railroads had spawned, interest in aviation was early and keen. By 1925 municipal leaders had decided to lease a former auto racecourse so that Atlanta wouldn't be left behind in the coming airplane age.

Pioneers and their successors worked so hard and so effectively that Hartsfield International Airport jockeys with Chicago's O'Hare for rank as biggest in the world. Measured in terms of space, Hartsfield is a clear winner. In 1985, takeoffs and landings at the Atlanta terminal topped the records at all other airports, anywhere. Analysts predict that 1995 will see one million flights logged.

Twentieth-century growth has transformed a once-small city into a burgeoning metro area with a population of more than 2.5 million. Political divisions, plus an always-strong base of black economic and professional leadership, have fostered the rise of strong and able black political leaders.

In the city that gave birth to Martin Luther King, Jr., multitudes endorse a slogan according to which Atlanta is too busy to engage in racial hatred.

Much of that busyness continues to be centered upon the city's

Population more than 2.5 million

role as a transportation center. Interstate Highways 20, 75, and 85 converge here. They are modern counterparts of the very early Old National Highway and of the Dixie Bee Highway (U.S. 41) that linked Chicago with Miami in early years of the auto age.

A "downtown connector" is formed where Interstate Highways 75 and 85 are briefly joined. Its path crosses what was once Sandtown Trail — one of the routes that converged near Standing Peachtree during Indian days.

Interstate Highway 285 was built as an outward perimeter. Now packed with the urban core of the metro area, it includes five intersections with interstate highways. These plus three inside the perimeter saw 1985 traffic flow of 395,753,742 vehicles.

"Spaghetti Junction," where I-85 North and I-285 intersect, has become an elaborate maze of long, curving entrance and exit ramps at many levels. This interchange is about as far removed from trails leading to Standing Peachtree as land transportation permits.

Communication developed simultaneously with transportation. Two telephones were installed in 1878; today Atlanta's toll-free dialing area is the world's largest — more than sixty miles long

Modern Atlanta, sprinkled with snow

and almost as wide, with 2,316,457 directory listings in 1986.

Less than a decade after the first crude telephone system was installed, the city adopted a new seal that depicts a phoenix rising from the ashes of Civil War destruction. Reborn Atlanta, or city of the phoenix, created the ultra-modern MARTA system of rapid trains plus buses. MARTA — the state-of-the-art urban transit system of the world — plays an internal role comparable to the external role of railroads, air lines and interstate highways.

Long proud of having encouraged migration from the North and East as well as from other parts of Dixie, Atlanta has ceased to be the Gateway to the South. Direct flights to South America, Europe and the Far East have made it a gateway to the world.

Business and political leaders have fostered both the image and the reality by which Atlanta moves toward the ranks of principal world cities of class No. 1.

First Train
From Terminus

Selection of a southern terminus for the proposed W&A R.R. did not trigger a land boom. Hardy Ivy and family, South Carolina natives who were the only permanent settlers, probably knew that a stake was driven by Stephen Long or under his direction. They considered it unimportant.

Two years later, in 1839, Ivy completed the purchase of land near his double-hewn log cabin. For 202½ acres he paid $225 — in farm produce.

At Montgomery's Ferry, eight miles away, more and more heavy wagons crossed the Chattahoochee. Most of them came from or were headed toward Decatur, seat of justice of fifteen-year-old DeKalb County.

Few of DeKalb's twelve thousand or so settlers were interested in the coming of a railroad. Only a handful of them had begun speaking of the spot selected by Long as Terminus.

Though the name stuck, a more logical choice would have been Junction. For before work on the W&A started, builders planned for it to connect with two other lines being constructed by private capital.

For the W&A, farsighted Georgia leaders had laid the credit of the state on the line to the tune of $350,000. It was a huge sum for

Arrival of the locomotive *Florida*

the era — but not enough. Roadbed preparation through 138 miles of Indian country proved to be slow and costly. Most of the money was gone by the fall of 1839 — and not a mile of track had been completed.

Backers of the Monroe R.R., later the Central of Georgia, were seeing more results. Their main line, already near Griffin, was pushing toward Terminus. In order for the two railroads to meet, a big embankment had to be built.

John Thrasher won the contract for the earthwork, so he quickly threw up a little store in the forest. He brought in laborers, mostly Irish, and for them built shanties with dirt floors. Most of them traded exclusively with him; few could afford regular trips to Decatur, the booming county seat. Though Terminus remained stagnant, by 1840 the county included eighty-four hundred free whites plus two thousand slaves and six free blacks.

All eyes turned toward tiny Terminus in December, 1842. A rail line had been completed all the way to Marietta and the first train would soon make a round-trip journey — including crossings of the awesome Chattahoochee River bridge.

In order to pull the first train from Terminus, the locomotive *Florida* was hauled sixty miles overland on a huge wagon pulled by sixteen mules. A passenger car, built at the state penitentiary

Iron depot and rail yard, 1887

in Milledgeville, and a freight car from the same source also came by wagon.

Few settlers in north Georgia had ever seen a locomotive. Many families drove their farm wagons to Terminus just for a look at the *Florida*. A few arranged to be included in the Christmas Eve excursion.

Spectators shouted themselves hoarse as the first train pulled away from Terminus; many discharged their firearms. At the river bridge the engineer kept a promise earlier made to passengers. He halted the *Florida* so that the fearful could walk across. After a ball in Marietta, celebrants returned to their starting point — the rough plank depot of the W&A, whose adjoining shed room offered hard liquor for sale.

No celebrant who made that round trip of forty miles imagined that, just four decades later, famous *Harper's Weekly* would send artists to depict their point of departure and return as the Gate City of the South.

By 1843, seven or eight families were living near Terminus. Having completed his grading work, Thrasher had sold out and moved to what he considered a better location. Stephen Long, who chose the place, had gone on record as hoping that it would some day be a good spot for a tavern and blacksmith shop plus a grocery.

Progress-minded settlers decided to scrap the name Terminus in favor of Marthasville — honoring the daughter of a former governor. About a year after that first train ran, they secured a charter for the renamed settlement. Five commissioners were to govern the one hundred or so residents.

Unknown to citizens of Marthasville, a West Point graduate stationed for a few months at Marietta had taken frequent long rides about the region. In the course of those rides, Lieutenant William T. Sherman had come to realize that — some day — the line of iron rails snaking northward from Marthasville would be of immense strategic importance.

Jeff Davis's Biggest Tactical Blunder

Residents of Marthasville — all two hundred or so of them — went wild on September 15, 1845. A train puffed into the village with ten cars of iron for the W&A. It had come 173 incredible miles — all the way from Augusta.

Settlers in the region had heard that one of the three projected railroads was about to be completed. Many came in covered wagons to see the first train arrive. According to its engineer, "campfires were gleaming in the woods" when it reached its destination.

Railroad builder J. Edgar Thomson, a Pennsylvania-born Yankee, had done the impossible. In remote Georgia he'd built and put into service the world's longest railroad. For just seven dollars, a fancy dude could ride first-class all the way from Augusta to Marthasville. He could take his horse along for an extra eight dollars and a two-wheel carriage for just six dollars more.

Chartered with permission to operate a bank as a sideline, the Georgia Railroad had a depot ready when trains started rolling. Long-standing tradition says that Thomson's dispatchers fussed and fumed. They found it a nuisance many times a day to write "Marthasville" on way bills and other papers.

J. Edgar Thomson   Martha Lumpkin

Probably on the spur of the moment, the man from Pennsylvania acted on their complaint by changing the name of the depot to Atlanta. Soon the depot was more widely known than the frontier village it served. Legislators began getting requests to make the coined named official.

On October 15 the post office became Atlanta. Late in December the name of an ex-governor's daughter was scrapped and the one-time town of Marthasville was chartered as Atlanta — probably a feminine form of "Atlantic."

Completion of a sawmill by Jonathan Norcross meant that the community now had industry as well as a functioning railroad. Collier's store and post office, opened a few months earlier, was universally regarded as superior to Thrasher's earlier commissary.

One year after the first Georgia R.R. train reached the southern terminus of the W&A, a locomotive pulled to Atlanta another train. This time it came on the 101-mile Macon & Western (later Central of Georgia). With long stretches of track unfinished and a tunnel to cut through a mountain, the W&A, though parent of the railroad town, would be third to reach it with a completed line.

Early use of the name Terminus had suggested that the W&A would start near Chattanooga and terminate a few miles from Decatur. But numbering of miles started at the south end. As a

Collier's grocery and post office

result, Atlanta's charter defined the town as including the territory within a one-mile radius of the Zero Mile Post of the W&A.

Election of Atlanta's first mayor in 1848 was followed by appointment of a board of health. Already there was eager talk of establishing a medical college. A frame building with a chimney at each end served as both schoolhouse and non-denominational place of worship.

When the 1850 census was completed, the growing town was found to number 2,572 persons — of whom only five hundred were slaves. Still, a suspected slave insurrection led to the arrest of nine persons. By action of the council, the city moved to begin collecting a one dollar tax for each slave sold at the Alabama Street Slave Pen. In order to live in Atlanta, a free black was required to post a two hundred-dollar bond. A slave had to get written permission to keep liquor at hand; for illegal possession, the penalty was thirty-nine lashes.

Completed after thirteen years, the W&A R.R. launched through-service between Atlanta and Chattanooga in 1850. By then the town whose site was selected by engineer Stephen Long had a telegraph office and a bank. Plans were already under way to make a bid to have the state capital relocated in Atlanta.

Fulton County was set off from DeKalb in 1853. As seat of the

new unit, growing Atlanta no longer had to look to Decatur in
order to conduct courthouse business. Establishment of a gas
works, medical school, flour mill and rolling mill gave civic
leaders a base from which to work for a new goal. Atlanta would
like to be the site of any central government developed by seced-
ing states, they said.

Though Jefferson Davis came for a grand reception, that bid
came to nothing. It was as a key supply center, rail hub and
hospital center that Atlanta was destined to become vital to the
Confederacy — so vital that Georgia R.R. engineer Lemuel P.
Grant spent months building a ring of defensive works that
guarded the city.

Completion of the eighty-seven-mile Atlanta and West Point
R.R. in 1852 meant that four lines converged at a single point.
With her central yard five tracks wide, Atlanta was the biggest
railroad center in rebel territory.

Small wonder that William T. Sherman led his troops toward
Atlanta in 1864. By early May it was clear that he planned to
mount a full-fledged Atlanta Campaign. Moving south, he
became increasingly dependent upon the W&A R.R. Every
week, about one thousand cars of ammunition and supplies
moved upon its rails.

Atlantans asked questions, fumed, prodded editors and wrote
letters to Confederate leaders. Everyone knew the W&A to be
single-track for long stretches. At the Chetoogeta mountain tunnel near Chattanooga, it was particularly vulnerable.

Why on earth didn't Davis send cavalry units to cut the W&A
at one or many points? Stranded because his supply line no longer
functioned, Sherman would be forced to abandon his march
toward Atlanta.

There was long-standing animosity between Davis and C.S.A.
General Joseph E. Johnston, as well as between Davis and Georgia Governor Joseph E. Brown. Some analysts think that the
Confederate President deliberately ignored chances to strike at
the W&A out of sheer malice. Others think it was lethargy that
led to inaction. Whatever the reason, failure to move against
sections of the W&A that were held by the enemy has been called
"Jeff Davis's biggest tactical blunder of the war."

Mystery Of
The Roswell Women

Ordered to sweep eastward and secure the bridge that crossed the Chattahoochee near Roswell, General Kenner Garrard tossed a question to his commander. "What shall I do with the town of Roswell?" he asked.

Sherman snapped, "Don't make a damned bit of difference. So you get out of here and go for rebels."

Slow grinding toward Atlanta by vast numbers of Union troops had brought them to Ruff's Station (now Smyrna) on July 4, 1864. After a brisk clash, Johnston's Confederates used darkness as a cover under which to pull back to fortified positions along the big river.

Even Sherman admitted that frontal attack would be futile. Until troops could be moved across the river in great numbers, there was no way by which he could strike directly at his target: Atlanta. Hence he sent Garrard and his men to Roswell, hoping to find the old bridge at that point to be usable.

Roswell owed its existence to the shallow ford of the Chattahoochee, crossed long ago by the old Hightower trail. Coastal planter Roswell King had dammed Vickery Creek in 1835 in order to get water power for a very early cotton mill.

By the time Yankees approached, Roswell had two cotton

Gen. Kenner Garrard   **Federal troops occupy Marietta**

mills, a woolen mill and the South's first apartment dwelling — a two-story structure built for mill workers.

Garrard's cavalry reached Roswell on July 5. Retreating rebels had burned the all-important bridge, but the village, of which federal forces knew little, was intact. All three mills were burned immediately.

Reporting to Sherman, the 1851 West Point graduate said he'd seized several thousand yards of cloth. One thing puzzled him, Garrard said. A French flag was flying over the woolen mill; debating alternatives, he'd decided that the flag was a rebel ploy. Ignoring the risk of an international incident, he had gone ahead with plans to torch the building over which it flew.

Sherman was enraged at the report. Any man hoisting the French flag in a move to protect rebel interests deserved to be hanged on the spot, he fumed. "Should you, under the impulse of anger, hang the wretch, I approve the act beforehand," he wrote to Garrard.

Then he followed with a long telegram authorizing his subordinate to "arrest all people, male and female, connected with these factories, and let them foot it, under guard, to Marietta, whence I will send them (by rail) to the North. The poor women will make a howl," Sherman noted. "Let them take their children and

Brick apartment house for factory workers, built in 1839

clothing, provided you have the means of hauling or you can spare them."

Meanwhile in Roswell, Union General Grenville Dodge — a railroad surveyor and engineer for whom Dodge City was later named — had his men at work. Using lumber salvaged from demolished buildings, they were throwing a new bridge across the river.

During a period of about seventy-two hours, Roswell women and some of their children were sent sixteen miles to Marietta. At least 350, possibly four hundred, rode in rough U.S. Army wagons or walked with the caravan along the approximate route of today's Georgia Highway 120.

"Only think of it!" began a dispatch by a reporter for the *New York Tribune*. "Four hundred weeping and terrified Ellens, Susans and Maggies transported in seatless and springless Army wagons, away from their lovers and brothers of the sunny South; and all this for the offense of weaving tent cloth and spinning stocking yarn!"

At Marietta, General George H. Thomas put the refugees into boxcars and sent them to Nashville. Following Sherman's orders, from that point they were to go to Indiana for resettlement.

Even in the emotional climate of civil war, editors questioned

Sherman's actions. Columns of the *New York Advertiser* lamented that a man in a major general's uniform had "so far forgotten the dictates of decency and humanity as to drive four hundred penniless girls hundreds of miles away from their homes." The *Cincinnati Commercial* labeled the capture of the females and children "a novel one in the history of war."

No formal justification of Sherman's deportation of the mill workers was ever offered by U.S. officials. Neither was there a follow-up report concerning disposition of them.

Notice of them in official records ends at Nashville. What happened to them afterward remains an unsolved mystery. Dozens of families, mostly in Indiana but a few as far away as Wisconsin, have vague oral traditions about arrival of females from the South during war years. Documentary evidence has not been found to support these traditions.

Twenty years after the mass deportation, editors of the *Confederate Veteran* magazine guessed that "few if any of these poor women ever saw their native soil again." That conjecture remains the bottom line; for practical purposes, several hundred Georgia women and children seem to have vanished as Union forces came into what is now metro Atlanta.

Busy with fortifications and railroads and hospitals and manufacture of war goods, Atlantans of the era probably knew nothing of what had happened a few miles away. Even had they known, it would not have prepared them for the coming siege, battles, surrender and destruction of the booming city that sprawled in every direction from a surveyor's stake driven into a forest glade just a quarter-century earlier.

Down But
Not Quite Out

About the time the last of the Roswell women reached Marietta on July 9, headed north, Johnston began pulling his forces across the Chattahoochee. Bridges were destroyed and his men retired into previously prepared fortified positions.

At some points, small trees had been skillfully woven together to form stout barriers. But in many spots the Confederate defensive works consisted only of loose piles of brush. Atlanta, nearly twenty miles south of the new battle line, was safe for now.

C.S.A. General Braxton Bragg, earlier removed from command for inefficiency, came to the rail center on a special mission for Jefferson Davis. He had been instructed to find out why Johnston had not stopped Sherman and, if necessary, to recommend drastic action. On July 16, three days after Bragg reached Atlanta, Sherman's army began crossing the Chattahoochee on hastily devised pontoon bridges.

Atlanta was placed under military government. That was nothing new; during a crisis period two years earlier civilian rights such as *habeas corpus* had been suspended for a time. Life had returned to normal after execution in the city of James Andrews and seven of his raiders who had managed to seize the locomotive *General* and race toward Chattanooga.

Gen. John B. Hood   Gen. William T. Sherman

Bragg spent hours with General John B. Hood, who castigated Johnston — his commander — for his policy of refusing to fight the Yankees and slowly retreating to fortified positions. Given the chance, Hood vowed, he'd quickly force the enemy into all-out battle.

After an exchange of messages between Atlanta and Richmond, Johnston was relieved of command and replaced by Hood. A spy slipped from the city and took the news to Sherman, who openly rejoiced. Hood would be much easier to lick than Johnston had been, he exulted.

Numbers and fire power, if nothing else, gave Federal troops a big edge. At the start of the push toward Atlanta, about ninety-nine thousand men in blue had 254 field guns. They were faced by no more than sixty-four thousand men in gray — who had only 144 guns. Slaughter at Chickamauga and at Kennesaw Mountain had left relative strength little changed. Sherman was ready to meet the rebels in hand-to-hand combat, anytime and anywhere.

Peachtree Creek was the place of the first big encounter, fought on July 20. Confederate strength was cut by forty-eight hundred men; Union losses ran to just eighteen hundred. Sherman's margin of strength was growing, instead of shrinking as Hood had hoped and expected.

From his Atlanta headquarters, the Confederate commander issued orders that led to a second big engagement on Friday, July 22. This time, fighting was so close to the city that the battle took its name. About seventy thousand men took part in the battle of Atlanta; Confederate losses may have reached ten thousand — against Federal casualties of just thirty-seven hundred.

Two major generals died that day — James B. McPherson on the Union side, and W. H. T. Walker on the rebel side. Atlanta Mayor Calhoun, who had already placed every able-bodied white male in one of the city's several military units, openly hoped that "Fighting Joe will do what Hood has not."

Georgia-born General Joseph J. Wheeler, head of Confederate cavalry guarding Atlanta, had earlier captured five hundred wagons full of supplies at Decatur. He was expected to avoid open battle but to strike frequently and hard at unexpected targets.

Hood's announced intention to meet the enemy in the open field, in full strength, was tested for the third time on July 28. Ezra Church proved to be his most humiliating encounter yet. Sherman's loss of about six hundred men cost Hood nearly five thousand of his seasoned veterans.

Confederates retreated inside Atlanta's heavily fortified defensive system; they had no other choice. Many civilians were sorry to see this move. According to English-born stationer S. P. Richards, the only resident who kept a detailed day-by-day diary, looting had started as soon as the city filled with soldiers.

Army wagons, soldiers and marauders had piled into Atlanta on the night of July 22, wrote Richards, "as though the whole army was passing through." Some of Hood's men broke into Richards' store. They stripped it of stationery, other paper and about thirty dollars in cash.

Yet the Atlantan by adoption realized that Yankees represented a threat far more serious than that posed by marauding rebels. For the first time in his life, he took up a rifle and served duty as a sentry. His wife and children moved their beds behind the chimney, hoping that would shield them from Federal shells that came from a distance and fell at random.

Piles of brush constituted many of Johnston's defensive works

Sherman had tentatively decided upon "a partial siege." Careful inspection had shown the vast defensive works that encircled Atlanta with few breaks to be too strong to assault and too extensive to surround. He would wait, hoping that Hood would venture another full-scale battle.

Though Atlanta had become an armed camp, there was little panic. Two of the city's four rail lines, leading from the south and the west, were in Confederate hands. Long trains brought hospital gear, essential supplies, and carload after carload of ammunition. There was ground for hoping that if Hood waged a defensive campaign, he could keep the enemy at bay until they would be forced to leave because their own supplies were exhausted.

In the entire Confederacy, only Richmond — the capital — had a defensive system as big and as strong as that of Atlanta.

Lemuel P. Grant, a native of Maine, had come South to work as chief engineer of the Georgia Railroad. He was placed in

A section of Grant's cheveaux-de-frise

charge of fortifying Atlanta in March, 1863.

Grant had no military experience but was a veteran engineer and builder. He requisitioned slaves from plantation owners, who were paid twenty-five dollars per month for each black furnished.

Slaves dug trenches, built redoubts and rifle pits. Instead of the clumsily and hastily built Chattahoochee fortifications of Johnston's troops, Grant erected many long sections of twelve-foot palisades. A defender could fire between these, but no attacker could squeeze through.

Spiked stakes, or *cheveaux-de-frise*, were built to protect major earthworks. Then trees were felled for about one thousand yards in front of defensive positions. With most redoubts planned to hold five big guns, artillery fire would have clear fields.

Using red mud plus slash pines plus slave labor, an engineer from Maine had made Atlanta relatively invulnerable to frontal attack. Roughly circular at a distance of about two miles from the starting point of the W&A R.R., twelve-mile defensive works created by the man from the North were too vast to be surrounded.

Atlanta's twenty thousand civilians realized that the city was down. But Grant's defenses and the troops of Hood and Wheeler, plus those all-important rail lines from the south and the west, promised that the rail center was not quite out of the fight.

Ruins As Far As
The Eye Could See

Unwilling to attack and unable to mount a full siege, Sherman pondered alternatives. To wait would lead, at best, to a stalemate. He decided to make Atlanta's two remaining rail lines priority targets.

While preparing to strike the Atlanta & West Point R.R. somewhere near Fairburn, he set out to give the city a never-to-be-forgotten drubbing. "One thing is certain," he said in an official report to Washington. "Whether we get inside of Atlanta or not, it will be a used-up community when we are done with it."

Big siege guns, plus fifty batteries of field artillery, began firing continuously on August 9. Since most shells fell at random rather than upon specific targets, casualties were suprisingly few. But civilians found life increasingly frustrating. In order to enter or leave the city — or move about the streets at night — a military pass was required. There was little time for anything resembling normal activities; all available manpower was needed for fighting the many fires produced by the bombardment.

Those families who could built stout little "bomb proofs," usually single-room dugouts into which everyone crowded when shelling was constant. Both food and water grew increasingly scarce. Many residents gave up and left Atlanta in order to take

"Bomb proof," built for protection from shells

refuge with relatives or friends at other points.

Hood exulted that most of Sherman's gunpowder and lead were being wasted; there was increasing ground to believe that the city could hold out forever.

At daybreak on August 26, Confederates defending positions on the old Sandtown road could hardly believe their eyes. One glance showed the trenches opposite them to be empty. Was it possible that Sherman had given up a hopeless assault in order to head North and rejoin one of the main bodies of Union troops?

That conjecture was quickly discarded. Scouts reported heavy movement of Yankees toward Red Oak. Soon there was word that the Atlanta & West Point R.R. had been cut.

Hood discounted these reports. Sherman would withdraw and the road would be rebuilt in a matter of hours, he insisted. There was no chance that men in blue would risk an all-out assault upon the Macon & Western R.R. at Jonesboro.

August 29 proved Hood to be dead wrong once more. Heavy fighting that began that day extended into the early hours of September. With about fifteen thousand men in the conflict, Union forces lost 170. Hood's twenty five thousand Confederates probably lost ten times as many. Jonesboro was occupied, tracks were torn up and railroad ties were burned to heat rails so they

Union tents near the center of Atlanta

could be bent beyond repair.

Atlanta was cut off from the rest of the world.

Late on the afternoon of September 1, Hood's troops began pulling out. Before leaving, they tried to destroy everything that could be of use to the enemy. An eighty-one-car train loaded with ammunition was burned; explosions and fires started by it leveled

81-car train destroyed by retreating Confederates

a huge rolling mill from which some of the plate for the ironclad *Merrimac* had come. Sherman could have the city — what was left of it, that is. Little good it would do him now.

Explosions heard by Sherman at Jonesboro told as clearly as though he'd received an official dispatch that all resistance was over. "Atlanta is ours, and fairly won," he reported to Grant.

Mobs began forming before the last Confederate troops marched away. Stores and homes were looted in what one civilian called "an uncontrollable outbreak of lawlessness."

Mayor Calhoun, unable to convene a meeting of the city council, resorted to use of a few leading business and professional men. Carrying a white flag, they rode to the nearest Federal unit. Acting without military authorization, Calhoun surrendered the city to Colonel John Coburn of the 20th Corps.

U.S. Army wagons began rolling into Atlanta shortly after noon. At the city hall, the Stars and Stripes were hoisted for the first time in four years. Grounds about that center became a tent city housing part of the army of occupation.

Sherman's Special Order No. 67, issued a few days later, stipulated that the city of Atlanta was exclusively required for military purposes. Hence, it must immediately be evacuated "by all except the armies of the United States and such civilians as may be retained."

More than four hundred Atlanta families — some still with black servants — began moving south on September 11. Sherman provided army wagons for use as far as Rough and Ready. From that nearby way station, refugees could go North or South as they chose. Editor George W. Adair of the *Southern Confederacy* newspaper was one of the last residents to flee. "On going up a big hill below Atlanta," he wrote, "the fire was blazing so brightly I could count the hairs in my horse's tail by the light."

Sherman himself now faced a dilemma of the first magnitude. By what means and route could he most swiftly and safely get his men back into Union-held territory while working as much havoc upon rebels as possible?

Though contemplated as an alternative earlier, it was in Atlanta that Sherman decided to send his men on foot and on horseback to the sea. At first, he probably planned to embark on Union

Last train prepares to leave Union depot before its destruction by Federals

Railroad station in ruins

gunboats once a port was reached. After cutting his telegraph lines and severing communication with superiors, he quickly saw that the devastation worked by his troops gave strategic importance to their escape plan. As a result, from Savannah he turned toward Columbia, South Carolina, instead of returning North by sea.

With Atlanta's bridges burned, her railroads and industries destroyed and block after block of business and residential sections smouldering, the March to the Sea began on November 15. Most of Sherman's sixty thousand men were gone before midnight; their commander waited until the next day to leave. Glancing backward from the outskirts, Yankees wrote home that they discovered "nothing but ruins, as far as the eye could see."

Headquarters For
An Army Of Occupation

In Atlanta, still badly war-scarred in spite of a start toward rebuilding, the Civil War ended April 30, 1865. From North Carolina, Joseph E. Johnston informed Georgia Governor Joseph E. Brown that he had surrendered the last large Confederate force to Sherman.

Union General J. H. Wilson was, for the moment, in command of the state. Few men — not even Sherman — were so despised. Leading troops toward Columbus, Georgia, he met only token resistance on April 16. Lee had surrendered a week earlier. Still, Wilson burned 115,000 bales of cotton plus four cotton factories, the Columbus arsenal and gun factory, three paper mills, fifteen locomotives and 250 cars, a rolling mill and immense quantities of supplies. A few days later at Macon, he issued a proclamation offering a reward of $100,000 in gold for the capture of C.S.A. President Jefferson Davis.

Brown called for an emergency session of the state legislature to meet in Milledgeville. Wilson responded by having Brown arrested — along with Alexander H. Stephens, Howell Cobb and Benjamin H. Hill. Georgia was organized as a military department, with district headquarters in Atlanta, Macon, Savannah and Augusta. Except for a provisional governor named by Presi-

Gov. Joseph E. Brown   Alexander H. Stephens

dent Andrew Johnson, most elected officials were permitted to
function. Yet final decisions rested with military officers headed
by General George H. Thomas — a key figure in the Atlanta
Campaign.

Still in office, Mayor Calhoun was given permission to borrow
money to operate the city. No one would lend it, so he issued
$20,000 in bonds. Ranging in denomination from twenty-five
cents to ten dollars, these bonds were for a time the chief medium
of exchange used in Atlanta business.

July 7 brought to the occupied city its most colorful commander. Prussian-born Prince Felix Salm-Salm, a professional
soldier, had come to America and joined the Union Army as a
colonel. While with Sherman's army at Dalton, Georgia, he had
become a brigadier general.

Princess Salm-Salm, Atlantans soon learned, spoke no German. She was the former Agnes Leclerq of Baltimore, called "a
cultured and high-spirited young woman" at the time of her
marriage to the soldier of fortune.

Scorning the sidesaddle that was then traditional among
females, Princess Agnes rode like a male. But her most spectacular accomplishments took place in bedrooms. From Governor
Richard Yates of Illinois she wangled for herself a captain's

**Princess
Agnes Salm-Salm**

**War-scarred downtown Atlanta,
1865**

commission and was regularly paid for "hospital service."

She was on intimate terms with General George B. McClellan, General Dan Sickles, General James B. Steedman and other key Yankee leaders. For her Atlanta home she selected one of the better residences not leveled by Sherman's artillery — the Lawshe house "on the west of the Peach Tree Street."

Princess Agnes was the only titled individual ever to be in a place of authority in Atlanta.

After the husband's brief tenure as post commander, Atlanta came under the heel of Major General John Pope. He reached the city, whose population was now back to the wartime peak of about twenty thousand, by special train. Coming as he did from

Chattanooga, he rode the rails of the W&A, re-built along with other lines by forces of the army of occupation.

Atlanta leaders welcomed him at the depot, escorted him to the National Hotel and threw a grand reception for him. He came by virtue of the Congressional Reconstruction Act under whose terms the city became headquarters of the Third Military District.

Pope signified his personal desire for reconciliation by wearing civilian dress for the reception given in his honor. Nearly two years earlier Atlanta had begun sending signals to the North. A mass meeting chaired by Mayor Calhoun had voted almost unanimously for a motion that deplored the assassination of Lincoln. Merchants indicated eagerness to restore commercial ties with the North, and citizens in general endorsed a resolution that called for "speedy restoration of all political and national relations."

Yet even the most eager reconstructionists were troubled by Pope's order of May 21. Under its terms, each senatorial district received an appointed team of voter registrars — two white males and one black male.

By October, many who had welcomed Pope to Atlanta didn't like to admit they had attended his reception. Newspapers "not friendly to reconstruction" had been deprived of printing orders from governmental units. Blacks had been given the right of jury service.

Worst of all, in the eyes of many, Pope had ordered an election designed to establish a convention that would frame a new state constitution. Among major cities of the state, white voters registered by newly-named boards exceeded blacks only in Atlanta. Even in the railroad center whose pro-northern ties caused downstate conservatives to castigate it, the outlook was bleak.

When the election started on October 29, it was gloomily and accurately predicted that at least three-fourths of ballots would be cast by blacks. Atlantans — and all Southerners — were beginning to realize that life would never return to pre-war norms.

A few persons found some solace in one provision of Pope's order of September 19, 1867. Under its terms, the proposed constitutional convention would not convene at the Capitol in Milledgeville. Instead, it would meet in his headquarters city, Atlanta.

New Capital Of
A Reconstructed State

Yankee military commanders dispensed patronage, which bought them the support of some native whites, or scalawags. Polling places at which blacks registered to vote were guarded by soldiers. With northern-born entrepreneurs added to the military-black-scalawag coalition, the power block so formed was unbeatable.

Pope's call for a three-day election to determine whether or not to hold a constitutional convention was largely ignored by conservative whites. Less than 107,000 votes were cast; more than 102,000 of them endorsed plans offered by the army of occupation.

Elected delegates did not assemble in Milledgeville, capital of the state. Instead 111 of them came to the city of Pope's headquarters, Atlanta. Scalawags were close to a majority, with fifty-three men in attendance. There were thirty-seven blacks, nine whites from outside the state and just twelve native-born white conservatives.

Convention leaders Rufus Bullock of New York and Amos Akerman of New Hampshire were eager to hammer out a new constitution acceptable to Washington. Along with it, they hoped to get approval to move the state capital to Atlanta.

Municipal leaders strongly backed the proposed move. To foster it, they offered to provide for the state a site and on it to build "a Capitol equal in value to the existing one."

Approval of the plan to relocate the seat of state government came on February 27, 1868. By then, Pope had been replaced by fellow West Pointer General George G. Meade — who had opposed Lee at Gettysburg.

Gov. Bullock

Meade learned that Atlanta civic leaders had made a formal bid to become the capital in 1847. When put to a state-wide vote in 1854, the proposal drew 49,781 negative votes and just 29,337 affirmative ones.

Like his predecessor, Meade wanted the governor and legislature to be at work close to his own headquarters. Long before votes were cast on March 20, it was clear that Georgia

Gen. Meade

Huts on lawn of future permanent Capitol

Opera house transformed into a costly Capitol

would, indeed, get a new capital city. Simultaneously, a newly drafted constitution was adopted.

Two candidates for the governorship, under terms of the new constitution, were disqualified by Mead. With many white males prohibited from voting because of their wartime activities, carpetbagger Rufus B. Bullock won the top civilian post.

For the new Capitol, Atlanta leaders provided their combination city hall and Fulton County courthouse, size seventy by one hundred feet. For weeks after the fall of the city, the lawn of this building had been crowded with huts of the 2nd Massachusetts Volunteer Infantry.

Georgia's elegant old Capitol in Milledgeville was vacated in favor of a commonplace little brick building. Within six weeks after the first legislative session held in it was launched, it was clear that a much bigger structure must be secured.

Music lovers of Atlanta had earlier started to erect an opera house five stories tall. When money ran out, Maine native Edwin N. Kimball picked up the unfinished building at a receiver's sale. He paid $31,750 for it and soon transferred title to his brother.

Kimball's brother, Hannibal, deeply involved in Reconstruction politics, saw the possibility of big money. He promised to provide Kimball's Opera House for use by the legislature for the session beginning January 1, 1869.

Soon he, too, was in financial trouble. His close associate, Governor Bullock, listened with sympathy when Kimball reported that he couldn't possibly provide carpets and furniture — not even heating and lighting apparatus.

During sixty days Bullock diverted to Kimball $54,500 in state funds — without the knowledge of Georgia State Treasurer N. L. Angier. That enabled legislators to work in a completed building that still belonged to Kimball.

In an 1870 deal, Bullock payed Kimball $250,000 for the former opera house. Simultaneously, Atlanta was ordered to pay the state $55,625 for the vacated Capitol in Milledgeville. Once the deal was settled, an old $60,000 mortgage on the opera house came to light. To prevent collapse of the entire deal, Atlanta bought the mortgage; later, the city had to cancel all claims against Kimball.

Altogether, the entrepreneur from Maine picked up at least $364,500 from property he had bought for $31,750. Lawmakers used the price-boosted structure for twenty years.

Long before the end of that period, Bullock had written out his resignation and had taken off for points north. He had every reason to fear impeachment by the legislature and preferred not to face charges.

Voters of the state, asked once more to respond to the issue of the location of the capital, turned down an opportunity to send it back to Milledgeville. Once that decision was made, lawmakers demanded that the Kimball Opera House be vacated in favor of a structure designed and built to serve as Capitol of the state.

Atlanta gave the site — ten acres of land where the old City Hall and Fulton County Courthouse stood. An architect was selected and a special building committee was named. Citizens got their first look at things to come on February 16, 1884, when the *Atlanta Constitution* published a six-column engraving that depicted the architect's rendering of the new Capitol.

When bids were opened, the contract went to the North. Miles and Horn of Toledo, Ohio, won the contract in September, 1884. They used Indiana limestone rather than Georgia marble for the

Cornerstone ceremonies, Georgia State Capitol, 1885

Capitol erected by Ohio building contractors

exterior and managed to complete the structure $118.43 under budget.

More than ten thousand persons crowded the grounds for cornerstone ceremonies on September 2, 1885 — the only phase of the construction captured in a surviving photograph. Many came from Macon, taking advantage of a special rail offer of a round trip for one dollar.

Earlier, after three separate "reconstructions" and ratification of the Fifteenth Amendment to the U. S. Constitution, Georgia was the last seceded state to win readmission to the Union, on July 15, 1870. Readmission came by virtue of the signature of President U. S. Grant, who had been commander-in-chief of Union forces during the Atlanta campaign.

Once a forest in which a surveyor's stake had been driven, Atlanta now sprawled over nearly nine square miles and claimed a population of more than forty thousand. A scornful observer guessed that "Confederate widows make up ten percent of the city's residents." Whether that was true or not, the new capital of the reconstructed state was determined to forget the past by devoting its energies to the growth-directed future.

Morris Rich
Chooses Atlanta
To Make A Start

Twenty-year-old Morris Rich, born in Kaschau, Hungary, as Morris Reich, was tired of riding horseback from Chattanooga in search of customers. He'd been selling for seven years; maybe it was time to let customers come to him . . . but where?

Having left Cleveland earlier, he rejected that region and surveyed "coming cities of the South." Atlanta, he learned, had in seven years rebuilt most of the five thousand structures destroyed during the war.

If Chamber of Commerce figures were to be believed, population had jumped 109 percent in the four years beginning in 1861. Business was said to be growing even faster, but the dry goods field was dominated by well-established firms. Something new would be needed — as well as capital with which to make a start.

From his brother William, already in Atlanta, Morris managed to borrow five hundred dollars. Late in May, 1867, he opened a retail store at No. 36 Whitehall Street after having covered mud holes with loose boards.

Before the first customer appeared at his 1,875-square-foot building of hewn logs, he adopted a basic policy: Anyone not satisfied with a purchase could return it with no questions asked.

Bidding for the farm trade, the merchant who had crossed the

Atlantic in steerage permitted barter of eggs, corn and other farm products for finished goods. Within a few days of opening, he bought his first newspaper ad. Pace of advertising in the *Atlanta Constitution* accelerated rapidly. Soon he was locally noted as the city's biggest advertiser.

Morris Rich

Another radical innovation was to offer all merchandise on "a firm one-price system." Most merchants of the era marked goods in code. It was taken for granted that once a price was divulged, customer and clerk would haggle at length.

That practice was time-consuming at best, and at its worst could be downright deceptive. Even the earliest ads placed by Rich were startlingly precise:

> Ladies White Cotton Hose, 10¢
> French kid gloves, 1 button, 50¢
> French kid gloves, 2 buttons, 75¢

Whitehall Street, viewed from Alabama Street, 1882

Joined by brothers Emanuel and Daniel, Morris made a series of short moves that ended at No. 45 Broad Street.

The first merchant in the Southeast to departmentalize his store, Rich reported seventy-five departments and eight hundred employees within two decades after his start on borrowed money.

From first-year sales volume of about $5,000, Rich's topped $647 million in 1985 from seventeen stores. Three more stores are now open. Richway, launched as a discount division in 1970 and now operating at more than thirty locations, is not included in that sales total.

Including branch stores (but not Richway), the business begun with $500 from a brother now employs more than eight thousand persons in more than 375 departments. Emphasis upon complete customer satisfaction, novel in 1867, is still basic to the enterprise Morris Rich launched.

He headed the business for fifty-eight years, never wavered in having chosen Atlanta over a dozen other potential sites at which to try to get customers to come to him.

Two years after Rich made his start in the rail center, work started on another line. Completed in 1874, the Richmond & Danville later became the Southern R.R. Atlanta's vast new Union Passenger Station was regarded as one of the nation's biggest and finest.

During the infancy of the mercantile enterprise launched by Rich, Atlantans built the splendid Kimball House hotel and DeGive's Opera House. In a single twelve-month period, 1871, four hundred structures went up.

Public transportation was launched that year, when the horse-drawn West End car line went into operation. By 1874 cars were running on the Marietta, Peachtree, Ponce de Leon Springs and Whitehall Street lines. Daring for its era, this early predecessor of MARTA built and used long trestles over deep creek beds.

Growth was so explosive that severe water shortages developed. Two private movements aimed at establishing a municipal water works failed. Hence, in 1870 the legislature authorized the City of Atlanta to borrow the money needed to build a system.

Using mostly convict labor, a dam was built on Peachtree Creek. Pipe lines were laid by a company headed by a son of

Lemuel P. Grant. Pumping equipment designed to provide three million gallons per day was purchased for $130,000.

Launching of service on September 11, 1875, included a public test of the system by firemen. They worked from hydrants at the Kimball House and the freight yard and soon announced that Atlanta's fire danger was greatly reduced.

They spoke too soon.

Morris Rich had, indeed, been accurate in identifying Atlanta as a growth center. Less than a decade after the fine new waterworks went into operation, it was hopelessly outgrown. In a bid to

Trolley starts across trestle spanning Clear Creek (now Ponce de Leon Avenue at Myrtle Street)

Artesian well at Five Points

ease the crisis for at least a few years, the city council authorized
the drilling of an artesian well.

A native of New York, John W. Baum, headed the construction
company that acted to relieve the water crisis. A 2,044-foot well
sunk by his crew was located at the intersection of Peachtree and
Marietta streets at a site where the Five Points flagpole was later
erected.

Many of the fast-growing stream of persons headed for the
emporium of Morris Rich stopped at the well for water before
proceeding with their shopping. Some of them were newcomers
who had reached the city by way of a fifth major railroad that
linked Atlanta with Charlotte. Proud builders called it the Air
Line because, straight as an arrow in many sections, it seldom
detoured to avoid natural barriers.

Eventually becoming a barrier itself between sections of the
city, the railroad gulch was conquered by viaducts. Now it provides a colorful and distinctive site for the central entertainment
district — Atlanta Underground Festival.

International Cotton Exposition Boosts City

Scanning out-of-town papers, the dynamic young managing editor of the *Atlanta Constitution* paused with the *New York Herald*. He reread a letter in it, and on August 29, 1880, Henry W. Grady reprinted a Yankee challenge.

Boston inventor and economist Edward Atkinson wanted to know why on earth persons having vital interest in cotton didn't get together. Exchange of ideas, he said, would benefit all.

Atlantans who read the reprint by Grady agreed that at least one Bostonian had a really great idea. What better place to implement it than here? But it should be global in scope, not just national.

London and Paris had held two great expositions each, but no international fair had been held in America. All the more reason for Atlanta to act quickly!

Late in the year a formal association was formed to plan and stage the International Cotton Exposition. Most officers were local, but the treasurer was Samuel M. Inman of New York City. As executive in charge, planners selected Hannibal I. Kimball.

In 1880, that choice was not innocuous. Most Georgians knew that Kimball was a native of Maine who came to Atlanta as a representative of the Pullman Company. He had managed to become chief lieutenant of reconstruction Governor Bullock — and to profit nicely from the relationship.

Yet there was little protest to the plan that involved putting Kimball at the head of the biggest enterprise Atlanta had ever undertaken.

Working with planners and dreamers, many of whom had been Confederate officers, Kimball proved his merits. For the expo to succeed, $200,000 had to be raised in advance — half of it from Atlanta. That goal

Hannibal I. Kimball

sounded ridiculous at first. But under Kimball's prodding, a six-hour campaign on March 15, 1881, yielded just over $100,000.

Oglethorpe Park, about two and one-half miles from Five Points and conveniently located on the W&A R.R., was made available by the city. While architects began making preliminary drawings, agents went to every state and to major cotton-producing countries overseas.

Formal opening of the expo came in October to the strains of Handel's "Hallelujah Chorus" rendered by six hundred voices. Shaped like a Greek cross, the main building was a model cotton factory 720 feet long and 400 feet wide.

Adults paid fifty cents admission, while children and students of all ages got in for twenty-five cents. An eight-minute run from the heart of the city on a special train of the W&A cost ten cents each way.

Day after day, full-page newspaper stories described activities plus exhibits from foreign countries and other states. Readers were frequently reminded that the Savannah cotton exchange was now second only to London's in size.

Mexican Veteran's Day, November 15, was especially dramatic. A former war-time resident of Atlanta — William T. Sherman — reluctantly made a short talk. It drew more applause than the speech of Governor Alfred H. Colquitt, aristocratic cotton planter and one-time Confederate major general.

Oglethorpe Park, 1881

International Cotton Exposition

Colquitt got a new suit at the expo, though. With Governor H. B. Bigelow of Connecticut, he had consented to be a guinea pig in an experiment that few persons other than Kimball expected to succeed.

Crowds gathered before daylight on October 27, publicized as promising a pair of "one-day suits." Shortly after sunrise, workers picked cotton from patches on the grounds. By 7 A.M., lint was being carded. Rushed by rail to a Fails & Jenks frame, it emerged as thread.

Then weaving began on a Crompton loom. Finished cloth went into dye vats and came out "black as night." One of Atlanta's favorite tailors cut the cloth into suits. H. H. Phelps of New York worked button holes at the incredible rate of two a minute.

At the climax of a glorious day, governors of Georgia and of Connecticut stepped on the platform, as alike as two peas in a pod in "handsome suits made from cotton that at sunrise dangled, dew-gemmed, from the stalks."

Those "one-day suits" made headlines around the world. But it was the set of exhibits from every state and seven foreign countries that pulled in visitors by the thousands until the expo closed on December 31.

World's Work magazine lauded it as "the most interesting exhibition ever held in this country." An analyst for the *New York Commercial Bulletin* judged that the expo marked the beginning of a new era for the South — "a formal abandonment of the past."

Editors in distant cities didn't know that two more Atlanta colleges were born in the year of the expo — Morris Brown and Spelman. Neither did they know that still another railroad, the Georgia Pacific, was pushing into the coal fields of Alabama.

Grady and Kimball, who were abreast of these local developments, stressed the international impact of the expo that was successful by every standard. They were right in hoping they'd helped to start Atlanta on the road to more than regional importance. But they were dead wrong in believing that cotton was the key to the future of the city and of the South.

An Atlanta Editor Invades And Conquers The North

Favorable publicity about the International Cotton Exposition caused its host city to be seen as symbolic of regional change. Atlanta was viewed as ready and willing to put the Civil War behind.

Henry W. Grady, editor of the *Atlanta Constitution*, was an eloquent spokesman for that point of view. Hence, he was in great demand as a speaker at gatherings in the North.

Members of the New England Society of New York sent him a polite note inviting him to be present at their 1886 banquet. They planned to offer a toast to "The New South" — a term coming into wide use — and hoped that Mr. Grady would be gracious enough to respond to that toast.

Though it didn't sound like an opportunity to express his full feelings, the editor accepted. He mulled over ideas but did not prepare a manuscript since his response would be spontaneous and brief.

At Delmonico's restaurant on Wednesday evening, December 22, assembled notables were eager to hear the speaker of the evening. Thomas DeWitt Talmage, pastor of First Presbyterian Church in the nation's capital, could be expected to be brilliant — and sensational.

He lived up to expectations.

To close his address, he gave an eyewitness account of the dramatic entry of Sherman's victorious army into Washington at war's end. When the stupendous cheering of listeners subsided, William T. Sherman was introduced from his place at the head of the table.

Members of the society, said newspaper accounts, "gave Sherman three times three and a tiger." When the uproar began to diminish, the master of ceremonies toasted "The New South" and gestured to indicate that Grady would respond for the region.

Unaware in advance that the conqueror of Atlanta would be an honored guest, the editor lauded the account of Sherman's return to Washington by Talmage. Earlier he had described "the foot-sore Confederate soldier returning home" to Atlanta — consecrated ground by virtue of "the blood of your brothers who died for your victory, and doubly hallowed to us by the blood of those who died hopeless, but undaunted, in defeat."

Grady twitted Sherman as "having been kind of careless about fire" and triumphantly reported that "from the ashes he left us in 1864 we have raised a brave and beautiful city."

By then, the journalist from the South had the Northern audience in the palm of his hand. His "response to a toast" became a spur-of-the-moment oration. Since he had no manuscript, the *Atlanta Constitution* couldn't print its editor's remarks until Christmas Day, after having received from New York "a full and accurate copy."

Having won his listeners, Grady told them that in the New South it was recognized that "the free negro counts more than he did as a slave." Blacks and whites must do more than raise cotton, he urged; they must raise farming supplies at home and process raw material.

In the New South, he warned, spinners of Massachusetts and ironmakers of Pennsylvania would be challenged.

Yet both Northern capital and Northerners themselves were cordially invited to aid in "the uplifting and upbuilding of the prostrate and bleeding South." In a single ringing sentence, Grady said, "We have learned that one Northern immigrant is worth fifty foreigners and have smoothed the path to Southward,

The Grady Monument in 1900

wiped out the place where Mason and Dixon's line used to be, and hung out the latchstring to you and yours."

Grady received a tremendous ovation from his listeners as well as rave notices in major New York newspapers. Though he did not coin the term and was not first to use it, his speech to the New England Society made "The New South" a famous and a lasting label for a changed society.

Most persons of the era believed that abandonment of some pre-war attitudes plus creation of cotton-centered industry would solve the problems of the South.

Skillful political leaders proved them to be wrong by drafting and adopting "black codes" that effectively wiped out many gains that seemed within reach of blacks during Reconstruction. Powerful economic forces, of which discriminatory freight rates were high on the list, made is impossible for southern industry to compete with northern industry.

Decades later, in a David-versus-Goliath contest, youthful Georgia Governor Ellis Arnall took on powerful Northern and Eastern railroad interests — and won. A 1944 decision by the U. S. Supreme Court abolished discriminatory freight rates and gave the South one of its biggest economic boosts ever. Earlier Arnall had succeeded in abolishing the three-dollar poll tax that effectively barred great numbers of blacks from the Georgia political process.

A full century after Henry Grady invaded and conquered the North, his city — and the region that includes it — has evolved from "The New South" to become "The Eastern Sunbelt," with the latchstring still out for Northern capital and Northern immigrants.

Hence, it is fitting that Grady's monument, erected soon after his 1889 death at age thirty-nine, depicts him standing near Five Points and gazing into the future in almost visionary fashion.

Gas Chandeliers
And Ten-Piece
Bedroom Suites

Henry W. Grady's famous New York City address elevated the concept of the New South into a nationally prominent symbol. Since his message was oriented toward the future, he said nothing about the fact that many fine Atlanta homes, with the Governor's mansion prominent on the list, were already equipped with gas chandeliers plus ten-piece bedroom suites.

Chandeliers owed their presence to Northerners who came to the rail center long before Grady verbally hung out the latchstring as an invitation to them. Ten-piece bedroom suites, mostly black walnut, were made available in quantity by the son of an Irish laborer.

Atlanta's earliest street lights burned whale oil and later kerosene. Citizens who lived nearby not only furnished fuel but also were responsible for lighting and extinguishing the dim beacons.

Savannah had been using coal gas for years. Augusta, Macon and Athens had scrapped their kerosene-burning street lights. Leaders of these cities laughed at the notion that a brash railroad junction could join the ranks of the gas-lit.

That really wouldn't have been possible without an influx of skill and money from the North.

Connecticut-born Julius A. Hayden came to Atlanta in 1835 at

Meter Wagon No. 2, Atlanta Gas Light Company

age twenty-five and married the daughter of a prominent land-owner. Later he formed a partnership with Connecticut native Thomas G. Healey. Brick from their kilns was used to build many notable early structures.

When Atlantans began to talk wistfully about how nice it would be to have streets lighted by gas, it was natural to turn to Hayden for leadership. He helped to form the Atlanta Gas Light Company and was elected as its first president.

But, in order to put gas to work, the company had to have a production plant plus a system of mains. For these, Hayden turned to still another Northerner — William Helme of Philadelphia.

An 1855 contract stipulated that the fledgling Atlanta Gas Light Company would provide gas for fifty street lights. Ornamental iron lampposts were bought for twenty-one dollars each; merchant John Tomlinson stocked and advertised fixtures suitable for use in offices and homes.

Christmas Day, 1855, saw ceremonial lighting of the city's first street lights that burned illuminating gas. These lights were dimmed only once, when Sherman — a Northerner of different stripe from Hayden, Healey and Helme — plunged Atlanta into darkness that lasted for months.

Rapid rebuilding of "the Phoenix city" from the ashes of war included erection of many bigger and finer homes in which gas chandeliers were standard. Electricity gradually replaced gas for illuminating purposes, but as late as 1905 the earlier fuel remained in use. Black entrepreneur Alonzo Herndon, who started the five-year building of his mansion that year, had it decorated with lions' heads from whose mouths gas flames spurted.

Alonzo Herndon

At the time of Grady's New South speech, ten-piece bedroom suites were much in vogue among Atlantans. A typical suite included a Gothic bed plus a bureau, a washstand with marble top, a towel rack, a rocking chair, a center table and four straight chairs.

Many families of ordinary means had one such suite — due to an innovation by J. J. Haverty. Competing with twenty older and larger business establishments, he launched the practice of selling furniture "on time."

His father, Thomas Haverty, belonged to a class of newcomers not exactly welcomed by Grady — if his remarks to the New England Club are to be taken at face value.

Thomas Haverty, one of thousands of victims of the Great Potato Famine, left Ireland in 1848. He docked in New Orleans, found work with the railroads, and made a number of moves that ended in Atlanta in 1852. Though the population was little above the two thousand mark, the town always offered a job to an experienced railroad hand.

After four years, Haverty had saved enough money to send for his wife, son and three daughters. One year after their 1857 arrival, a second son was born.

James Joseph Haverty — always simply J. J. in later life — was five years old when he learned to run for the family "bombproof" at the sound of approaching artillery shells. His sixth birthday came just two weeks after Sherman burned Atlanta.

Working first as a "cash boy" and then as a clerk for John Ryan & Company, he managed the carpet department of M. Rich & Bros. before deciding to open a furniture store of his own. Haverty had saved $600. That persuaded President John W. English of the Lowry Bank to lend him six hundred more. With it, he built a twenty-five- by seventy-five-foot store on Hunter Street and stocked it scantily — keeping his job at Rich's as security.

J. J. Haverty

Within three years he had sold enough bedroom suites and other furniture to begin expanding. Before the turn of the century, he had opened stores in St. Louis, Kansas City, Memphis, Little Rock, Hot Springs and other cities.

With long-time partner A. G. Rhodes, the furniture dealer erected the Rhodes-Haverty Building just before the Great Depression. It was Atlanta's tallest structure until a bank building topped it in 1955.

Still fully alert and very active at age seventy-seven when the Haverty Company celebrated its fiftieth birthday, J. J. sent a note to Margaret Mitchell congratulating her upon impending publication of *Gone With The Wind*.

In a note penned on her thirty-sixth birthday, one of the world's favorite novelists chided Haverty. "You —," she said, "and not I — should be writing a book about Atlanta!"

J. J. never wrote that book. But the company he launched with $1,200 now has sixty-nine showrooms in forty-one key cities of ten sunbelt states.

Newcomers to today's metro area often find it puzzling that there are so few native Atlantans. Many are first- and second-generation Americans like Haverty, with roots in Europe or

Early trolley, Fair Street to Grant Park line

Africa or South America or the Orient. Others are Notherners or descendants of Northerners who acted upon Henry Grady's open invitation.

Most other residents seem to have come from elsewhere in the state or region. Electric trolley cars joined gas chandeliers and ten-piece bedroom suites in 1889. They replaced the pioneer street railway system that once used 114 mules, plus a later one that employed four steam engines. Building of electric trolley lines was the work of Alabama native Joel Hurt.

Even Henry Grady was not a native. He spent his youth in Athens, studied in Virginia, and made a success of a Rome, Georgia, newspaper before deciding at age twenty-two to join the crowd and make Atlanta his home.

Orator Booker T. Washington

Cheers And Jeers For "The Atlanta Compromise"

Ex-slave Booker T. Washington, described as "a gentle man with big, strong hands," bowed to the audience before stepping to the podium. There was an electric air in the Negro building; no black had ever before been invited to address political and economic leaders of Atlanta and of the South.

Polite smiles acknowledged a vivid introductory anecdote about thirsty seamen. Lost for many days, said Washington, men signalled an approaching vessel in an appeal for water. They were told, "Cast down your buckets where you are!" Perplexed but responsive, they obeyed — and found that they were sitting in the fresh water of a huge river's mouth.

Members of his race must act as did thirsty seamen, the speaker insisted. "It is in the South that the Negro is given a man's chance in this commercial world."

Interrupted by an ovation that was repeated many times before he ceased to speak, the head of noted Tuskegee Institute hammered out what came to be remembered as "The Atlanta Compromise."

Under its terms, Negroes of the South were urged virtually to retire from political life — and to play humble and menial roles in commerce and industry. That was the necessary price, said Wash-

Cotton States and International Exposition of 1895

ington, for the white man's good will and patronage.

Listeners on the opening day of the Cotton States and International Exposition of 1895 cheered themselves hoarse. Newspaper accounts praised Washington as "the first Negro ever to electrify a predominantly white Southern audience."

Many blacks who read brief excerpts from the speech or who heard about it at second- or third-hand responded with quiet jeers. Some labeled Washington an "Uncle Tom" and withdrew their support from the Alabama manual school he headed.

At the Expo, reconciliation between North and South was dramatized by an encampment that started on September 21. Confederate veterans for a few days lived and slept in tents alongside those of members of the Grand Army of the Republic.

W. E. Du Bois, destined in 1896 to become the first black to win a Ph.D. from Harvard, was already in correspondence with Atlanta University officials. Soon he came to that institution as professor of economics and history.

Segregation, discrimination and racial violence were growing worse rather than better, Du Bois insisted. Terms of "The Atlanta Compromise" might temporarily ease some tensions but in the end would widen racial gaps and reduce blacks to legalized equivalents of slavery.

Piedmont Park, about 1900

Publicly repudiating the philosophy of Booker T. Washington, by 1900 the Atlanta educator and colleagues founded a movement that became the National Association for the Advancement of Colored People. Du Bois was labeled "the voice of black protest."

Despised as the NAACP and its leader were by hosts of persons throughout the nation, not simply in the deep South, Atlanta was the logical headquarters for such a movement. Population was approaching ninety thousand, putting it behind only New Orleans and Louisville in the entire South. About forty percent of Atlantans were black; many belonged to the emerging professional and business class.

Though the campus of Atlanta University was small and bleak, more and more of its dapper graduates were self-consciously upward bound. Seven males made up the class of '94. Three of them became college presidents; a fourth was father of a pioneer black lawmaker. Florida-born James Weldon Johnson won international recognition as a poet and playwright and is still famous for his volume entitled *God's Trombones*.

Launched in November, 1865, the educational institution was initially sponsored by the American Missionary Association. Classes were started in a boxcar purchased for $310.

One century after Booker T. Washington urged compromise that amounted to capitulation on many fronts, Atlanta University is the world's largest predominantly black higher educational complex. It includes Morehouse College, Spelman College, Clark College, Morris Brown College and the Interdenominational Theological Center.

Combined enrollment of institutions that make up the university complex is more than eight thousand. No program offered is remotely comparable to Tuskegee Institute's early focus upon manual arts and semi-skilled trades.

Yet "The Atlanta Compromise" rolled out in what is now Piedmont Park by the president of Tuskegee had great merit at the time. Noted sociologist Gunnar Myrdal, in his classic volume *An American Dilemma*, insists that Booker T. Washington must be appraised from the perspective of his era.

Whites who cheered so heartily at the Cotton States and International Exposition, says Myrdal, did not fully realize that the black speaker was "the supreme diplomat of the Negro people through a generation filled with severe trials, who was able by studied unobtrusiveness to wring so many favors from the white majority."

For many blacks in 1895, favors were better than nothing. For a majority of whites, limited concessions were a reasonable price for racial harmony.

Atlanta University, 1895

Atlanta University's Class of 1894

"Brother giving water to fallen brother"

World's Largest Painting Is A Yankee Legacy

New York native George V. Gress, widely known as lumber king of Georgia, couldn't pass up a bargain — whether he had any use for it or not. With railroad contractor Thomas J. James, he attended an 1889 auction sale of a bankrupt circus. They bought it, since James could use the railroad cars and wagons.

Gress gave the circus animals to the City of Atlanta. Officials promptly made plans to place their "costly and rare collection" at the park donated by Lemuel P. Grant and bearing his name. Now the city of 65,533 — 42.9 percent black — had a zoo.

During months that followed, the first unit of a municipal hospital named for Henry W. Grady was dedicated. A golf course was built, and J. W. Alexander brought an automobile to Atlanta.

Gress spotted another bargain in 1893. An immense painting of the Battle of Atlanta, somewhat damaged, had changed hands several times. Bought for $1,100 and placed on view in a Grant Park building, it was deeded to the city in 1898.

Herr Wilhelm Wehner, moving spirit behind creation of the 17,430-square-foot painting, launched his American Panorama Company in Milwaukee. Some of his artists, along with *Harper's Weekly* veteran Theodore Davis, came to Atlanta to depict the furious action of July 22, 1864.

German artists who painted gigantic battle scene

Their finished work, entitled "Logan's Great Battle," is believed to have been intended to foster political ambitions. Major General John A. ("Black Jack") Logan was an 1884 candidate for the vice-presidency.

When McPherson was killed near Atlanta, it was Logan who took over his troops. As U.S. Senator from Illinois, he was a manager of the impeachment trial of Andrew Johnson. Later he was a key figure in formation of the Grand Army of the Republic and for six years was its commander in chief.

Though "Black Jack" was prominently featured in the huge painting, it didn't win him the national office he sought. Owners sent it on a tour, and crowds paid to see it in Detroit, Minneapolis and Indianapolis during closing years of the 1880's.

Paul Atkinson of Madison, Georgia, bought the work of art at an 1890 auction sale. He exhibited it in Nashville and in Chattanooga, then brought it to Atlanta. Public interest was disappointing.

With revenue dwindling by the month, Atkinson found a buyer in Florida. H. H. Harrison had great plans to take "Logan's Great Battle" to the Chicago World Fair of 1893 but balked when told he'd have to erect a brick building to house it.

Still in Atlanta, the painting was damaged when heavy snow

Old Abe, with members of the 8th Wisconsin

crushed the roof of the building in which it was stored. Owners of the lot on which the damaged building stood gained ownership of the painting as satisfaction for a $937 judgment; it then passed into the hands of Gress.

Numerous other immense dioramas, usually painted in five segments, had been executed. Civil War scenes were especially popular. Most artists who worked upon them were Europeans who spoke little or no English.

Total historical accuracy was not a priority requirement; purchasers wanted viewers to come in large numbers and pay for admission. No wonder, therefore, that Atlanta's world-famous battle scene includes a vivid but imaginative portrayal of a Yankee soldier giving water to a fallen Rebel — said to be his brother.

Even the famous war eagle, Old Abe, is depicted as having been seen hovering over the Battle of Atlanta. Mascot of the 8th Wisconsin Volunteer Infantry, the big bird was present at thirty-eight engagements but never took part in a Georgia battle.

Noted artist Wilbur G. Kurtz, who restored the great war painting several decades ago, expressed doubts about the presence of Old Abe. But he refused to meddle with a masterpiece and left the eagle in the painting.

Lemuel Grant

Gustav Berger

Wilbur Kurtz

By the time it was placed on exhibition in Atlanta, the painting that extolls Logan was one of the few of its kind that survived. A companion piece, also once owned by Paul Atkinson, depicted the storming of Missionary Ridge. Though long popular, it deteriorated with time and was scrapped.

Lauding a native of Ohio and given to the City of Atlanta by a New Yorker, the war painting went into a circular building — or cyclorama — designed especially for it.

Restoration was supervised in 1921 by an artist born in Illinois

Hand-to-hand fighting, as depicted in the Cyclorama

New Jersey locomotive *Texas*, before restoration

and reared in Indiana. Kurtz also took charge of WPA workers who, during the 1930's, added three-dimensional figures to the foreground.

Still another restoration was supervised by Gustav A. Berger — born in Vienna, Austria, and working out of studios in New York City.

Refurbished and rehoused by Atlanta at a cost of more than eight million dollars, the painting that depicts one of the city's darkest days is annually visited by persons who come great distances to see it.

Also housed in the Cyclorama is the restored locomotive *Texas*. It was this wood-burner that railroaders used to chase and eventually to overtake the stolen locomotive *General* in April, 1862.

For decades, the mechanical hero of *The Great Locomotive Chase* sat on a siding and rusted. When placed in the basement of the then-new 1927 Cyclorama building, it was in deplorable condition. Since it was state property — part of the rolling stock of the W&A R.R. — Governor Richard B. Russell wanted to give it away in 1931. Members of the Atlanta City Council balked and refused to permit its removal from the Cyclorama. Restored by a team led by Colonel James G. Bogle, it is a priceless survivor of the Civil War.

Despite the presence of a now-gleaming historic locomotive, Atlanta's Cyclorama remains Southern only in locale. For when purchased by the W&A in 1962 for $9,050, the *Texas* puffed southward as a splendid example of craftsmanship by a builder whose shops were located in New Jersey.

Neiman-Marcus Grubstake Comes From Growing Atlanta

Atlanta's growth was accelerating by the time another Yankee's gift pushed the city into erecting a special building to house the world's largest painting. It was growth that caught the eye of Louisville-born Herbert Marcus and his brother-in-law Al Neiman, a native of Chicago.

Both ambitious youngsters had sales experience; both thought Atlanta looked good. For the moment, though, Neiman couldn't resist the pull of Manhattan. They organized the American Salvage Company, with Al heading it in New York City. Herbert and his bride opened an Atlanta branch in 1906. As promoters of special sales, they learned how to attract buyers by use of banners, flamboyant signs and band music.

Herbert and Minnie Marcus soon reported that they were right — the city of their choice was full of action. A few years before their arrival, one-time C.S.A. General John B. Gordon had brought twenty thousand Confederate veterans for an encampment. Months later, Northern steel magnate Andrew Carnegie had selected Atlanta for a $145,000 gift with which to launch a library bearing his name.

Paderewski had appeared at the Grand Theater in 1900. Within the decade, a visit by Geraldine Ferrar would trigger plans to

Construction at Marietta and Broad Streets, 1901

bring the Metropolitan Opera to the city.

Opening of the Whitehall Street viaduct five years before the arrival of Herb Marcus was a big step toward bridging the gap between two business districts. That all-important railroad gulch separated north Atlanta — smaller but growing — from the busy south side until a series of viaducts was built.

Expansion of trolley service, temporarily inconvenient, had led to resurfacing of many streets. Soon the Georgia Power Company would acquire existing systems and launch a program of expansion.

Railroads were still booming. Service had been launched by the Georgia, Carolina, and Northern line a decade earlier. Now the elegant new Terminal Station permitted easy passenger change from one line to another.

There was one cloud on the horizon; it brought a furious storm about the time that the American Salvage Company was organized.

Election of Hoke Smith to the Georgia governorship on a program of black disenfranchisement triggered the race riot of September, 1906. With at least five thousand persons engaged in street fighting, ten blacks and two whites were killed while seventy others were injured. With population at or near 150,000

The elegant Terminal Station, 1905

— 33.5 percent black — whites had started the riot, according to a Chamber of Commerce finding.

In spite of racial tension and a nationwide economic slump, the Atlanta branch of the American Salvage Company grew rapidly. So rapidly that Al and Carrie Neiman abandoned New York City in order to join forces with Herb and Minnie Marcus.

One product the sharp young salesmen promoted would later enable Asa G. Candler to build a concrete warehouse said to be the biggest in the world. His 1905 Candler Building was already a marvel of size and ornamentation. Candler's secret-formula Coca-Cola, being sold in bottles, was sweeping the nation.

Business of Neiman and Marcus grew so rapidly that it attracted attention of potential buyers. They had two offers, recalls Stanley Marcus, chairman emeritus of Dallas-based Neiman-Marcus. They could swap their profitable salvage company for Coca-Cola stock and a Missouri or a Kansas bottling franchise, or they could pocket $25,000 in cool cash.

They chose the cash. With the grubstake acquired in Atlanta, they opened the Outer-Garment shop in Dallas, specializing in ready-to-wear. Since Carrie Marcus Neiman had experience in blouse sales, she was active in the business from the start. Average age of the four when their store opened was twenty-six;

three of them were high school dropouts.

Neiman-Marcus was already world-famous when the Atlanta store opened in 1972 as the second out-of-Texas branch. With unusual architecture and original sculpture, the 120,000-square-foot mart was widely lauded for its "glittering, airy theme."

There would have been no Neiman-Marcus had young entrepreneurs who got off to a fast start in Atlanta chosen to accept Coca-Cola stock in payment for their American Salvage Company.

Health Care Foundation Puts Atlanta In Limelight

Long-time railroad executive William G. Raoul never got over the early death of his daughter, Rosine. In a fashion almost like that of Don Quixote, the Atlantan without medical training set out to dethrone the killer disease that had taken his daughter.

In a one-room office, Raoul launched the Atlanta Anti-Tuberculosis and Visiting Nurse Association. His 1907 goal: mastery of what had been considered "a Northern disease" until the era of the Civil War.

Raoul visited the North to learn what he could about tuberculosis. He inspected the tiny New York shack of Dr. Edward L. Trudeau, regarded as the nation's first sanatorium. Then he came home and put up a one-room frame structure at Alto, Georgia.

William G. Raoul

Before it was completed, he saw that it would be too small. That led the railroader to push for establishment of Battle Hill, designed to serve Atlanta and Fulton County.

His program was not only one of the earliest aimed at a specific malady; it also put Atlanta into the limelight because of its work among blacks. At his death in 1913, the man who had headed the Mexican National Railroad for seventeen years left a will that established a foundation to fund health care.

His bequest — fifty thousand dollars — was big money in 1913. Today it helps to fund the work of the American Lung Association of Georgia. Public awareness of Raoul's pioneer foundation and its work was a factor in boosting Atlanta's growing role as a health center.

While it was still only a railroad village, some of Atlanta's leaders had started to talk of launching a medical school. It got under way in 1855 and by 1859 had 156 students. Heroic work saved the buildings of Atlanta Medical College from the torch when Federal troops destroyed most of the city.

Very early, the altitude of Atlanta made it a haven for persons fleeing yellow fever. During war years, many public buildings and some private homes were converted into field hospitals. Two Sisters of Mercy arrived from Savannah in 1880. Their "institution for the sick and afflicted" — St. Joseph's Infirmary — became the city's first permanent hospital.

Tax-supported Grady Memorial Hospital opened two years later. Now among the nation's largest, its services range from emergency service to a foster grandparents' program.

Georgia Baptist Hospital opened in 1901; three years later, Methodists set out to build a facility. That's how Bishop Warren A. Candler came to announce a challenge pledge on Christmas Day, 1904. If churchmen would match it, said he, his brother Asa would contribute $12,500 toward establishment of a fifty-bed Wesley Memorial Hospital (now Emory University Hospital).

Full significance of William Raoul's gift is realized only when it is compared with the health-care pledge of Coca-Cola magnate Candler. There are reasons to believe that generosity of the railroader influenced Charleston, South Carolina, native Thomas Egleston. Three years after the Raoul Foundation was funded, Egleston left the bulk of his estate — $400,000 — to launch a children's hospital that opened in 1928.

With the Egleston bequest still very much in the news, Dr.

Early Grady Hospital ambulance

Joseph Goldberger of the U.S. Public Health Service dramatically chose Atlanta as the site for the future Centers for Disease Control.

Born in Czechoslovakia and reared in New York City, the Jewish physician had challenged "the Southern disease" and had won. Instead of being spread by bacteria as generally thought, Goldberger convinced his incredulous Atlanta audience that pellagra was due to dietary deficiencies and, hence, was easily preventable.

Today both tuberculosis and pellagra are very low on the list of maladies afflicting Americans. The Henrietta Egleston Hospital for Children is nationally renowned. Emory University's medical school faculty and graduates, plus its hospitals and clinics, provide about one-third of the metro area's health care. Because the federal Centers for Disease Control is located here, public health specialists throughout the world continually look to Atlanta for help. Established with a goal of achieving malaria control, the agency that has become the CDC is the only major federal program with headquarters outside Washington, D.C.

Dr. Joseph Goldberger, Thomas Egleston, Asa G. Candler and the Sisters of Mercy would be inordinately proud of movements they helped to launch. Could she tour health facilities of the metro area today, little Rosine Raoul would register her top-level pride at the way her daddy used his money long ago.

Atlanta Football:
Stuff Of Which
Legends Are Made

"An almost inconceivable score of 222 to 0 was piled up by Georgia Tech's Yellow Jackets," headlines in the *Atlanta Journal* of October 8, 1916, informed readers. Sports writer Morgan Blake exulted that it was a world record, sure to stand for a decade.

Blake was wrong only in his time estimate. For years, the *Guinness Book of World Records* has devoted major space to a game played before a crowd of less than one thousand spectators. Changes in rules make it unlikely that Tech's world record will ever be broken.

Assistant coach Bill Alexander may have been partly responsible for the incredible score. Two days before the squad coached by Ohio-born John W. Heisman was due to be host to Tennessee's noted Cumberland squad, Alexander reputedly boasted, "If we don't win by fifty points, we ought to lose."

Halfback Everett "Strup" Strupper responded instantly: "If we score one hundred, will you set 'em up for the gang, Alex?"

"Nope," Alexander replied. "But if you make two hundred points I'll set up the varsity, the scrub and the frosh."

That was all an already fire-eating Tech squad needed. Drawn from a student body of 843, the Yellow Jackets faced opponents

Georgia Tech vs. Cumberland University, 1916

from a school of about five hundred to six hundred students —
who had been 1907 All-Southern champions.

Heisman, who also coached baseball, cut the water allowance
for his players during the week before the game. In typical
Heisman fashion, he ordered football players to eat their meat
nearly raw.

No one then anticipated that the coach who spent fifteen years
in Atlanta would reach the tail end of his career in New York City.
There he worked as athletic director for the wealthy but not-so-
athletic Downtown Athletic Club.

Well-heeled members of that club put up the money to establish
a trophy in the form of a two-foot bronze runner stiff-arming a
tackle. It was to be presented annually to the outstanding college
football player in the nation. Called the Downtown Athletic Club
Trophy, it was labeled the D.A.C. by fans.

That was in 1935.

Before the trophy was awarded for the first time, Heisman
died. Admirers insisted that his name be attached to the award,
which is how a one-time Tech coach gained a kind of immortality
that is afforded to very few.

As members of his squad went through warm-up exercises in
preparation for their 1916 meeting with Cumberland players,

Heisman wasn't thinking of an award or a trophy. Morgan Blake kept reminding him — and newspaper readers in general — that at the start of the season he'd bragged, "We at Tech are determined to show folks that it is no very difficult thing to run up a score."

With a touch of October chill in the air, his players made good. Muscogee County native "Strup" Strupper scored forty-eight points with eight touchdowns. Jim Preas of Johnson City, Tennessee, made only three TD's — but in the first half alone kicked eighteen "goals," as they were then called. He racked up a total of thirty-six points — one more than Tommy Spence.

Tech made twenty first downs to Cumberland's none. Tech gained 501 net yards rushing to Cumberland's forty-two. Not counting kickoff returns, the Yellow Jackets moved the ball 959 yards; Cumberland had a net loss for the game of twenty-eight yards.

John W. Heisman

Gen. Leonard Wood

It was strictly ground action — pure old-fashioned bone-crushing football. Not a pass was thrown. Officials called the game after seven and one-half minutes of the fourth quarter; had they not done so, the score might have gone to three hundred.

Old grads, faculty members and players alike were stunned by the 1919 announcement that Heisman was leaving Tech — involuntarily. He and his wife had decided to divorce, so they brought in mutual friends and divided their assets.

In his best Shakespearean manner, the coach who had moonlighted as an actor announced that they couldn't live in the same city any longer. "It's her choice. If she decides to stay in Atlanta, I'll go," he said.

Which is how Heisman left the city and a record of winning teams. Had his wife preferred to live in Cleveland or Atlantic City, who knows what additional records would have been chalked up by Heisman's players?

First played in Atlanta in 1892 at Piedmont Park, intercollegiate football got off to a great start when Auburn walloped Georgia 10-0. Interest accelerated the following year when Tech met Georgia.

Dr. Leonard Wood, who had come to the city as post surgeon at Ft. McPherson, rode his horse to the site that became Grant Field and served as combination trainer/player for Tech. Listed simply as "Wood," his identity was discovered, and angry Athens fans tried to stop the game. Resumption of play — with Wood still on the field — led to a 28-6 victory by Tech.

Years later, General Leonard Wood, Chief of Staff, U.S. Army, sent a telegram to Atlanta's Ivan Allen, Sr. It resulted in establishment here of a major base for World War I training.

No event of the era spawned more local interest than did Atlanta football — briefly outlawed by the city council after a game at Brisbane Park in 1897. There a Georgia Bulldog died as a result of gridiron injuries. That dark hour was separated from the never-to-be-equalled victory of Heisman's squad by less than one generation.

Could any early eleven have stood up against a modern team? Regardless of how that question is answered, there's no argument on one score: Early Atlanta football was the stuff of which enduring legends are made.

Fort Mac: Nerve Center
Of U.S. Combat Readiness

Atlantans who had long referred to the city's U.S. military base as "that Yankee garrison" sat up and took notice in mid-April, 1917. From pages of the *Atlanta Journal*, they learned that six companies of infantry would be reassigned to Fort McPherson.

Many citizens didn't like the news. Scuttlebutt — which soon proved to be correct — had it that the incoming soldiers would guard German prisoners of war.

Crew members of the German ships *Kronprinz Wilhelm* and *Prinz Eitel Friedrich* were the first prisoners to reach Atlanta. By the end of June, 419 were in the city. Prison population peaked at 1,346 in June, 1919.

Military leaders assured fearful citizens that prisoners presented "practically no threat"; besides, they were under constant guard. But relaxation of rules led to establishment of five-man work gangs, each with a guard. Anxiety mounted in the city when it was learned that more than one hundred gangs were unloading concrete and wheeling rock for construction of Camp Jesup, an adjunct to the fort.

Not a single incident marred the two-year stay of prisoners, who competed for a chance to do manual labor at twenty-five

German POW's at work for twenty-five cents a day

cents a day. At war's end, a few elected to live in Atlanta or other U.S. cities. Tensions eased when the last contingent set out for Germany aboard the *S.S. Rotterdam* in September, 1919.

Never a fort in the conventional sense, McPherson is a well-developed military reservation. Its roots go back to antebellum days, before "Yankee" became an expletive.

Georgia legislators decided that the 101st battalion of the state militia needed a place at which to drill. They selected a pasture belonging to Whitehall Inn owner Charner Humphries and put it to good use.

C.S.A. authorities took charge of the old muster and parade ground after Georgia's secession. Barracks plus a cartridge factory, built on the site, boosted Atlanta's importance as a military center. When the city fell, retreating Confederates burned the factory and most barracks to prevent their use by Union troops.

As headquarters for the Third Military District, U.S. Army of Occupation, Atlanta badly needed quarters for officers and men. Under General John Pope, a start was made toward construction of a ten-company post. His successor, General George G. Meade, saw the completion of McPherson Barracks on fifty-three acres of leased land.

James B. McPherson, the dashing young Union brigadier

Iverson Gate, McPherson Barracks   **J. B. McPherson**

general who died in the Battle of Atlanta, was honored in the
name of the installation. Yet the main entrance, Iverson Gate,
commemorated C.S.A. General Alfred Iverson. Of Federal
officers who fought here, only McPherson is commemorated, but
at least a dozen streets of the base were given the names of
Confederates who made futile efforts to save Atlanta.

Reporting upon an inspection of McPherson Barracks in 1870,
the U.S. Surgeon General was highly complimentary. He particularly liked the altitude — "1,084 feet above low-water mark at
Savannah, Georgia."

Each barrack, he noted, measured 156 by twenty-seven by
thirteen feet and provided each of sixty-seven men with 727 cubic
feet. Single bunks were equipped with straw ticks. There was no
washroom or bathroom — but long troughs had been built under-
neath each barrack "for the purpose of washing."

A two-story hospital had three portable bathtubs for use of
patients. In addition, this building boasted "a privy in the rear —
provided with boxes sliding under the seats, into which dry earth
is thrown daily." Boxes were emptied every night, said the
Surgeon General.

Soon after the post was given this glowing description, the
U.S. Secretary of War ordered that it be abandoned. Buildings

Spelman College faculty and students before Union Hall, converted from barracks, 1881

World War I draftees de-train in metro Atlanta

were sold at public auction. Some of them were bought by the American Baptist Female Seminary — later Spelman College. Though formally abandoned by the military, the vicinity of the old post remained popular as a summer camping area. Troops stationed in yellow fever country especially liked to come to Atlanta for a few weeks at the height of the fever season. Prodded perhaps by popularity of the site for encampments, Congress took a timid step in 1885. For purchase of land on which to establish a new ten-company post and for erection of new barracks, lawmakers appropriated fifteen thousand dollars. Many of the buildings erected with part of that money are now listed in the National Register of Historic Places.

By 1889 the installation was formally named Fort McPherson. Soon it became a general hospital, as well as a place of confinement for a handful of prisoners taken in the Spanish-American War. Along with Camp Gordon in DeKalb County, the fort was a major training center for World War I draftees.

World War II saw it serve again as a major hospital center, supply depot and center for both reception and separation of 200,000 military personnel. Fort Mac then settled for a time into the routine of a small peacetime post.

Dramatic changes started in 1973 with reorganization of the U.S. Army's structure. A new major headquarters, the U.S. Army Forces Command, was established at the Atlanta base. FORSCOM concentrates on combat readiness of forces throughout the United States and its possessions. Because it is the largest combat headquarters in the free world, FORSCOM is often called "Pentagon, South."

Initially created for use by soldiers of the army of occupation, Fort Mac is one of the region's biggest hidden industries. Annual economic impact of the base that commemorates a gallant Yankee who died in an attempt to capture Atlanta is about $250 million — and rising fast. Multitudes of civilians in the metro area hardly know that the base exists; military strategists everywhere know that it is a crucial element in the U.S. military establishment.

Asa G. Candler

Bishop Warren A. Candler

"Coca-Cola U" — Methodist Response To Vanderbilt

Coca-Cola tycoon Asa G. Candler wrote a long and momentous letter on July 14, 1914. He addressed it to, "My Dear Brother" — Bishop Warren A. Candler, head of an educational commission named by Methodists.

After deprecating his wealth as popularly viewed, the soft-drink maker stressed the need for church-sponsored higher education. Then came the heart of his message: an offer of one million dollars as endowment to launch for the Methodist Episcopal Church, South, "an institution of University grade east of the Mississippi River."

That offer was triggered by a court decision.

Much earlier, Methodists had established Central College in Nashville and had upgraded it to university status. Trustees accepted from transportation magnate Cornelius Vanderbilt a gift of $500,000 in 1873. Simultaneously, they changed the institution's name to honor the Northern benefactor — who later doubled his gift.

Outraged churchmen, angry at seeing the university become independent, sued to recover what they considered to be their property. Years of litigation ended when their claims were thrown out. That left Methodists of the South without a university.

Warren A. Candler's commission, charged with replacing lost Vanderbilt, received and considered offers from Birmingham, Atlanta and Washington, D.C. His brother's offer settled the issue. Once Atlanta was chosen as the site, Bishop Candler was unanimously elected first chancellor. With a theological school given top priority, classes were launched in Wesley Memorial Church late in September. Leaders envisioned use of Wesley Memorial Hospital in conjunction with a proposed school of medicine.

A new university was in the making, but where was its college of arts and sciences?

At Oxford in Newton County, about twenty-five miles away, Methodists had launched a manual labor school in 1834. It did not prosper so was upgraded to college status and named for recently deceased Bishop John Emory.

Fifteen students, all trained in the manual labor school, entered Emory College in 1838. Three of them won diplomas in 1841.

Trustees of Emory College offered that institution as the undergraduate unit of the embryo university. Acceptance of that offer, with the Oxford campus retained, led to use of the existing name when the university was chartered in 1915. Simultaneously, Atlanta Medical College joined the institution as its third division.

With Atlanta's population approaching 200,000, the downtown locations of theological and medical departments were regarded as less than suitable. Peachtree and other major streets were carrying more and more traffic. Asa G. Candler came forward once more. His Druid Hills Company, a land development enterprise, offered a tract of about seventy-five acres — far from the city — as a campus.

A few carping critics growled, "Candler stands to make a lot more money from development of Druid Hills than he gave to start the university."

Theology moved from downtown to a stunning marble building in the Italian Renaissance style; a year later in 1917, some departments of the school of medicine went to the new campus. When the first marble dormitory was built, it was given the name of Samuel C. Dobbs — nephew of Asa Candler. As sales manager

Dobbs Hall, Emory University

for the Coca-Cola Company, Dobbs had pushed the Atlanta firm into the top rank of American advertisers.

Small wonder that most students and an occasional faculty member typically referred to the institution as Coca-Cola U.

Neither that nickname nor an occasional objection to the way in which Coca-Cola money was shaping the university had any impact upon trustees. Long ago, Emory College had faced and had weathered worse situations.

In 1880, President Atticus G. Haygood had startled rural Newton County by publicly calling for better treatment of blacks. Orators of that era typically eulogized heroes of the Lost Cause, damned the Yankees and pronounced a blessing upon antebellum Southern life.

Haygood — anticipating by nearly a decade some emphases made famous by Henry Grady — called for forward orientation, rather than backward. He listed weaknesses in the social structure of the South, with provincialism and illiteracy heading the list. "The true golden age of the South is yet to come," he said.

Haygood's message reached New York financier George I. Seney, who sent Emory College $50,000 — the first big money ever to come to Georgia from the North. Many who learned of the gift and of the building erected to commemorate it used expletives in speaking of the Methodist college and its leaders.

Earlier it was the ownership of the slave girl Kitty by Bishop James O. Andrew of Oxford that triggered the North/South split in the Methodist Episcopal Church.

So Emory University trustees ignored objections and went after all the Coca-Cola money they could get. Direct contributions by the company are estimated to have been about $2.5 million. Huge as they were for the era, gifts by members of the Candler family have since been eclipsed by those of Robert Woodruff and his close relatives.

Total Coca-Cola money poured into Emory University is in the range of $250 million. It has brought slow but significant changes. Financial independence has caused ties with the church to be weakened; Woodruff's absorbing interest in medicine long ago pushed the primary concern of founding fathers — theology — far into the background.

Now often characterized as seeking to become the prime Southern rival of Harvard and Yale, the university largely shaped by Atlantans in the past is a significant factor in shaping Atlanta of the future.

"Welcome South, Brother" Gains New Impact

"The *Atlanta Journal* is authorized temporarily to broadcast weather reports ... station must use radio call letters WSB ... repeat WSB."

Opening lines of a March 15, 1922, telegram meant a new era for Dixie. Sent from the U.S. Department of Commerce, the dispatch came collect. It reached Atlanta just two years after Pittsburgh's then-dominant KDKA was assigned the nation's first regular call letters.

Under terms of its temporary license, WSB was barred from broadcasting market reports. "News, entertainment, and such matter" could go out on a frequency different from that used for weather reports.

Augusta-born Major John S. Cohen, president and editor of the newspaper, was sure that the radio-phone had a future — this in spite of the fact that consoles, or receivers, sold for $700 and up. Pushed by Cohen, WSB went on the air the night that telegram was received. Two ninety-foot towers and an antenna had already been erected on top of the newspaper building.

Broadcasting began with one hundred watts of power. Equipment was so limited that opera star Rosa Ponsell — making her radio debut in Atlanta — hit a high note one night and blew out

WSB director Walter Iler (left) with operator Walter Tison

the transmitter. Still, Henry Ford had his first encounter with radio when he donned a headset and listened during a visit to WSB.

Walter Iler, who had picked up skill during a stint in military service, was station director. WSB's only other employee at start-up time was federally-licensed operator Walter Tyson.

Musical groups such as Byron Warner's "7 Aces" were big hits. So were skits by Ernest Rogers and Lamdin Kay, who tried to do anything a listener suggested.

That was only right, said Rogers and Kay, because their fans had selected the slogan linked with sterile call letters assigned by the U.S. Department of Commerce. A contest had brought suggestions that ranged from "We Shoot Bull" to "World's Super Broadcaster." Such ideas as these didn't have a chance when the railroad-born slogan of "Welcome South, Brother," was submitted.

Kay formed the nation's first radio fan club, WSB Radiowls. On the air, he offered a certificate naming a listener as "Honor Outpost for WSB, the Voice of the South." Stacks of telegrams requesting certificates came from all over the South.

Super-promoters Rogers and Kay staged the nation's first radio wedding before WSB was a year old. Henry Bagwell and Grace

Buice spoke their vows into micro-
phones, while listeners as far away as
Birmingham oohed and aahed.

North of the Ohio River, publisher
James M. Cox had been a candidate
for the presidency — with F.D.R. as
running mate. Disappointed at failing
to gain the White House, he had
begun to expand his newspaper hold-
ings. Late in the 1930's he bought the
Atlanta Journal — with WSB as part
of the package.

James M. Cox

Cox infused big new capital into
the radio station. As a result, wattage jumped from one hundred
to fifty thousand — the maximum then permitted. Then, in 1948,
after a long delay, WSB gained a license to operate a television
station.

Cameras and microwave equipment plus a mobile unit had
already been purchased — waiting for FCC approval to go on
line. Seventeen years earlier, the federal agency had turned down
WSB's request for experimentation in this field. Federal officials
notified Atlantans then that they "did not want radio with pictures."

Internally labeled "The Eyes of the South," WSB-TV got its

The "7 Aces" orchestra

go-ahead just four months after Nelson Ream bought Atlanta's first TV set. By the time the station went on the air as Dixie's first in September, 1948, the city boasted about twenty-five hundred viewing sets.

Little more than a decade later, there were so many radio and TV stations in operation that business analysts pronounced the market to be saturated. Somehow that assessment failed to impress yachtsman, billboard company operator and born gambler Ted Turner.

When he launched WTBS as "Superstation Channel 17," some industry observers snickered. Long before his news team scooped the world in Iraq, it was clear that his challenge to the established networks was giving their executives second and third thoughts. Acquisition and colorization of old movies, plus production of brand-new material, has brought the city of Ted Turner into the league whose only players were once New York and Hollywood.

Former Governor of Ohio James M. Cox made the *Atlanta Journal* the flagship of his growing newspaper chain. Today Cox Communications, Inc., operates eight TV stations, twelve radio stations and twenty-four cable TV systems in addition to newspapers.

Transportation was the key to Atlanta's early growth; today the city is a multi-media communications center. Air waves of the city, regarded as nearly saturated long ago, now carry programs of all major radio and TV networks plus educational radio and TV. Privately owned stations have proliferated along with cable services.

Even the future of the telephone is deeply involved with what was once a nearly-desolate railroad junction. Fiber optic cable was first tried here on a commercial scale, with such success that the metro area includes American Telephone & Telegraph Company's huge fiber-optic manufacturing plant — biggest in the world.

Rebecca Felton
Topples Barriers

"She'll never be seated. Tom Hardwick is trying to pay off a political debt the easy way."

That widespread verdict on the part of voters was ignored by eighty-seven-year-old Rebecca Felton of DeKalb County. She'd either be the first female U.S. Senator or she'd put up such a fight that Washington would look as though the British had come back to finish the demolition job they started in 1814.

Old-time political leaders snickered. They hadn't been totally surprised at events following the death of Senator Thomas E. Watson in September, 1922. In such circumstances, it was normal for a governor to name someone to fill the unexpired term — knowing that the appointee would never take the oath of office. It was unusual for a woman to be named . . . but Felton was an unusual woman.

As a member of the Presidential Advisory Commission, she had access to the nation's head. Surely he'd call a special session at which she would become a senator, if only for a couple of months.

Absolutely not, said Warren G. Harding. He did not think women had any place in politics — not even at the ballot box.

Rebuffed by the president, the Atlanta woman took a different tack. Walter F. George, a courtly Southern gentleman of the old school, had been elected to a regular term in the seat left vacant by Watson. On November 21 he could withhold his credentials for a day. That would challenge Senate leaders to decide whether or not to let an appointed woman sit there. He agreed to do so.

On the fateful day, Mrs. Felton appeared in a black dress and bonnet. There were no fireworks in spite of world press coverage. She charmed some who had vowed they'd never alter for sixty seconds the structure of "the most powerful all-male body in the world." Those whom she did not charm, she bowled over.

Senate rules were temporarily suspended. For the first time, a woman took the oath of office as a U. S. Senator. Minutes later she rose to speak.

Peering at fellow senators through her granny glasses, Rebecca

U.S. Senator Rebecca Felton, age 87

Atlanta suffragettes' parade, 1913

Felton told them, "The women of this country are on the move. They will no longer consent to be treated as second-class citizens."

She did not, of course, foresee that a few generations later the tables would be so completely turned that in many situations a female candidate for an office or a job would have an edge over equally qualified males.

Impoverished in girlhood by after effects of the Civil War, Rebecca Ann Latimer became active in public affairs. After her marriage to Dr. William H. Felton, she was a major factor in his successful campaigns for election to the U. S. Congress.

Campaign experience having convinced her of the power of the printed word, she became a regular columnist for the *Atlanta Journal* in 1899. During twenty-eight years in which she wrote that column, she campaigned for one unpopular cause after another — and usually won. She fought for abolition of the system by which convicts were leased as laborers, for adoption of state-wide prohibition, and especially for women's suffrage.

Though derided by cartoonists, suffragettes paraded annually in Atlanta from the turn of the century until passage of the Nineteenth Amendment to the U. S. Constitution. Their League of Women Voters, formed during years of controversy, remains a powerful political force.

Not all gains by women of the Felton era were in the political arena, though. Peachtree Street was set on its ears in 1920 when Geraldine Ferrar did a strip scene in the opera *Zaza*. That was only a few months after Marian Anderson had received her very first concert fee — fifty dollars — from Atlanta University.

Symbolic though her one-day term as U.S. Senator was for Rebecca Felton and her contemporaries, her formal admission to the lawmaking body meant that one more very big and very high barrier had toppled before an Atlanta woman.

Isidor Straus
Turns Atlanta
Toward The North

Newspaper headlines of March 13, 1925, informed readers that the famous R. H. Macy department store was coming to Atlanta, by way of a merger. Isidor Straus, head of the New York firm, had reached agreement with executives of the Davison-Paxon-Stokes Company and leading bankers.

Plans called for a gigantic new store whose construction would be handled by the Asa G. Candler Company. Two aspects of the venture really startled most Atlantans.

Though the new Davison's would be just six stories high, they'd be unlike any in the city. Floor-to-ceiling specifications were such that the sidewalk-to-roof height would equal that of the eleven-story Henry Grady hotel. That meant the new Davison's would be the world's tallest six-story building — a far cry from the early Macy building at 204 E. 14th Street in New York.

For reasons few veteran city watchers fathomed, Macy's head had decided to move from Davison's old location at No. 57 Whitehall Street. Almost unbelievably, the long-established retail district would be abandoned in favor of a site well north of the railroad tracks.

Vital as those tracks were to the early years of the settlement that had become Atlanta, they were now divisive. Viaducts

Davison-Paxon Company, 1927, a unit of Macy's

spanned the railroad gulch, but the region immediately north of it had not been favored for retail business. To move out of the area of high traffic was risky, indeed.

Straus and his colleagues did all they could to make sure that business would follow them north of the tracks. Something new to Atlanta would be included in the new store — a nonprofit vaudeville theater.

Artisans came from Italy to place fine ornamental plastering. A thirty-seven-foot penthouse on top of the building became the city's highest point. Long before the grand opening on March 21, 1927, passers-by had gawked at the largest expanse of display windows in the world. They stretched 620 feet along Peachtree, Ellis, and the arcade at the north end of Davison's new home.

For Atlanta, it was a turning point. Other merchants moved into the area, many from south of the railroad tracks. Once started, the northward trek has never slowed down.

For Macy's president and his relatives, it was a homecoming of a very special sort.

Lazarus Straus came to the United States from Bavaria in 1854.

He operated a small store in Talbotton, Georgia, then moved to Columbus. Civil War disruptions sent him North with his sons, Isidor and Nathan.

Earlier, Isidor had gone to Europe as secretary to Lloyd G. Bowers of Columbus. Bowers planned to buy British ships with which to break the Union blockade of Southern ports. His mission failed, however, and he returned to Georgia. Straus stayed in England as a broker in Confederate

Isidor Straus

bonds; at news of Lee's surrender, he sewed $10,000 in gold into a garment much like an undershirt and sailed for Philadelphia.

Isidor was surprised and somewhat dismayed to find his family living in Philadelphia's Merchants' hotel. He persuaded them to go with him to New York, where they soon bought a crockery firm and moved it into a twenty-five-by-one-hundred-foot space in the basement of R. H. Macy's store.

Crockery sales were so good that in 1888 the Straus family bought 45 percent interest in Macy's and 5 percent more in 1891. By 1896 they were sole owners. Lazarus had long before turned over most of the business to his sons; Nathan and Isidor made Macy's the world's largest department store.

Nathan won prominence as a leader in the fight for pasteurization of milk; Isidor went down on the *Titanic* in 1912. It was his namesake who brought Macy's top management team to Atlanta and arranged for the Straus family to return to Georgia roots by purchasing Davison's and relocating the store.

Later it was briefly identified as Davison's/Macy's before in the 1980s the downtown store and all other units of the chain became simply Macy's. As Straus anticipated half a century ago, the main growth has been toward the northern metro area.

But before the department store head envisioned that pattern of growth, a colorful educator surprised supporters by selecting what was at the time "the far northeast" as the site for a college campus.

Mr. & Mrs. J.T. Lupton steer for Oglethorpe ground breaking

Launched near Milledgeville and named for Georgia's founder, Oglethorpe College was a Civil War casualty. At least two early attempts to reestablish it in Atlanta failed. Then came South Carolina native Thornwell Jacobs, who envisioned Atlanta as the growth center of the South.

Jacobs decided to build in the style of Oxford University's Corpus Christi College. For the reborn Oglethorpe University, he accepted beautifully wooded but isolated land far out on Peachtree Road. Critics said he had lost his mind.

Chattanooga Coca-Cola bottler J. T. Lupton didn't agree with that verdict. He made an initial gift of $100,000 and, aided by his wife, steered the mule-drawn plow that broke ground for the university that was deliberately far from Five Points. Lupton then poured $10,000 a month into Oglethorpe's operating budget for years. Publisher William Randolph Hearst liked the reborn school and its isolated location so well that he gave $250,000 plus six hundred acres of priceless California land.

Continuing northward growth of metro Atlanta has brought once-remote Oglethorpe University within easy distance of a MARTA station and its fast trains. Macy's headquarters is solidly downtown, close to high-rise hotels and office buildings that rose as the city grew past the store.

"Lone Eagle" Gives Atlanta Aviation A Mighty Boost

Atlanta went wild on October 11, 1927.

With the entire world bidding for a glimpse at the man who first flew nonstop across the Atlantic Ocean, Charles Lindbergh spent a day in "The Gate City of the South."

Ordinary folk went to Candler Field, under lease by the city, for a glimpse at the man who was revered as "The Lone Eagle." Then they proceeded to Tech's Grant Field for afternoon ceremonies.

Alderman William B. Hartsfield smiled so broadly for so long that one account said "it looked as though his face would crack." One of those relatively rare citizens who was born in Atlanta and spent his entire life in the city, Hartsfield paid a 1909 visit to the auto racetrack owned by Asa G. Candler.

At the Hapeville race course dubbed the Atlanta Speedway, nineteen-year-old Bill spent only a few minutes watching cars before he became fascinated by a French monoplane that staged a show, then landed. Hartsfield soon began taking lessons and learned to handle a plane well enough to fly with barnstormers of the era.

Hartsfield was, therefore, the logical man to head Atlanta's aviation committee at its creation in 1923. Within three years, the

Candler's Atlanta Speedway hoped to rival Indianapolis

committee scored a triumph of first magnitude. Airmail service between Atlanta and Miami was launched by the U.S. Post Office.

That venture lasted less than three months, however. No fields were lighted, and even during daylight hours planes of the era couldn't move mail as rapidly as did fast night trains.

Federal officials let it be known that a New York to Miami mail route was under consideration. In order to win a place as a stopping point on that long route, an airport had to be equipped for night flying.

Birmingham, Alabama, was keenly interested. Insiders said that the city had a built-in advantage because beacons could be located on peaks near the airport.

Bill Hartsfield heard of a highly advanced lighting system that had been developed in Holland. Then he persuaded fellow members of the city council to find money to put that system at Candler Field. He was then ready for the feds — but still needed a groundswell of public support.

Writer Harold Martin once called Hartsfield "the great promoter, the colorful con man who above all else loved politics, his city, and its people."

Only a person with such a combination of qualities would even have dared to go after Charles A. Lindbergh. Scores of bigger and more important cities wanted him; what did "little ole Atlanta" have to offer?

Hartsfield counted upon memories of the past.

He knew that Lindy had purchased his first plane, a government-surplus

William B. Hartsfield

"Jenny" of World War I vintage, at Souther Field near Americus. That was in 1923. In that plane, Lindy first tried his wings — in Georgia — four years before becoming a world hero.

"Colorful con man" Hartsfield used all his wiles. To the astonishment of political rivals and the delight of the masses, he announced that the *Spirit of St. Louis*, piloted by Lindbergh, would land at Candler Field less than five months after having touched down at Le Bourget Field, Paris, at the end of a solo flight across the sea.

Atlanta's celebration in honor of Lindbergh has never been topped, except by the premiere of *Gone With The Wind*. Lindbergh Drive was named for the aviator as a lasting tribute.

Many members of the public saw Lindbergh and his history-making plane. Multitudes more read column after column about the visit in newspapers. Public enthusiasm generated in this way cinched the federal deal that was already under discussion.

Properly lighted at what Hartsfield acknowledged to be "no small cost," Candler Field won out over Birmingham's field. That made Atlanta a key point in the new network that linked Miami with both New York and Chicago.

Harold Pitcairn was one of the first persons to fly the night mail through Atlanta. A company he founded built the first big hangars at Candler Field — and developed into Eastern Airlines.

Hartsfield persuaded the city to give up its lease in 1929 in order to purchase Candler Field for $94,500. It was a rash step,

The Spirit of St. Louis (center foreground) in Atlanta

though foreshadowed by action of the city's merchants just prior to the outbreak of the Civil War. Speaking for then-tiny Atlanta, merchants had dared to ask that their town be designated a U. S. port of entry — for the benefit of rail shippers.

Aviation enthusiast Hartsfield became mayor of Atlanta in 1937. Then and many times later, he checked election returns in offices of the *Atlanta Journal* — initial home of radio station WSB. Though once defeated by a margin of eighty-three votes, he bounced back and for a quarter of a century "ran the city as though he owned it." Airport expansion was always close to the top of his list of priorities.

While living, Hartsfield wouldn't listen to proposals that his name should be permanently attached to buildings or parks — though he couldn't prevent zoo supporters from calling a zesty young primate "Willie B." At his 1971 death, Mayor Sam Massell directed that the municipal airport be named William B. Hartsfield International.

Completion of new facilities in 1980 made Hartsfield the world's largest passenger terminal complex. Its 138 gates can accommodate, simultaneously, up to 109 widebody aircraft. With assets of more than $1 billion, the municipal airport was in 1980 designed to handle up to fifty-five million passengers a year.

Initially considered "another fine example of bragging, Atlanta style," the title "international" was more hopeful than realistic when bestowed. Yet 1986 saw the start of construction aimed at doubling the number of gates for international travel. With seven new gates added to six in use, Hartsfield's capacity to process international passengers will jump from twelve hundred to three thousand per hour.

July, 1986, also saw "international" gain new meaning by means of a 6,958-mile link between Atlanta and Tokyo. Japan Air Lines began billing the city Sherman didn't quite destroy as an "American gateway to the Far East." During the first two months of flight by 340-seat jets, J.A.L. showed an in-flight movie: *Gone With The Wind* — with Japanese sub-titles.

If Lindbergh could make a return visit, he'd find Hartsfield hard to believe. In lieu of a former auto speedway in the middle of what were once cow pastures, he'd find Atlanta's runways and hangars surrounded by parking lots with space for seventeen thousand autos — filled to capacity and running over, much of the time.

Martin Luther King, Jr.

MLK: Prophet Of Non-Violent Social Change

"Son, I want you to do something for me when I'm gone," said James Albert King. "Big Mike," as he was known in the family, promised that he would honor the deathbed request whose nature he did not know.

"Change your name from Michael to Martin," his father instructed. "Change Little Mike's, too."

It was a request that King was glad to honor. He'd never liked the name Michael, selected by his mother. There were Martins in the family lineage, and the name was crisp as well as sturdy. About a year later, when "Little Mike" was five, the legal changes were made. As a result, the boy became Martin Luther King, Jr.

Had his grandfather wanted one of his own names to be perpetuated, the child would have become James Luther or Albert Luther. Instead, the dying man had specified the only name that would lock into Luther to become charged with symbolism.

Impact of that decision, though beyond measurement, was clearly potent.

Mrs. Coretta Scott King's account of her husband's life includes memories of a scorching day in Chicago. More than fifty thousand persons were gathering at Soldier Field to hear an address by Martin Luther King. In preparation for it, the two of them and their children went to City Hall — closed and locked because the day was Sunday.

"In a magnificent symbolic gesture that rang down the centuries from his namesake," she recalls, "he nailed his demands to the closed door of City Hall — just as the German Martin Luther had nailed his ninety-five theses to the door at Wittenberg."

Musing about the best time to live in his last public address, the prophet of non-violent social change considered alternatives, then concluded: "I would go by the way that man for whom I am named had his habitat. I would watch Martin Luther as he tacked his theses on the door of the church."

Martin Luther, Jr. — sometimes still "Little Mike" within the family — grew up in a middle-class black community within an expanding Atlanta. He was not yet a year old when the city annexed five suburbs. With area of 179 square miles, the new population total of 270,366 made it the second largest city of the South and twenty-second largest of the nation. More than ninety thousand blacks formed a cohesive society that rivaled in size and exceeded in economic opportunity most such enclaves in big Northern cities.

Lacking such an established constituency, it would have been impossible for William A. Scott to establish *The Atlanta World* — destined to become the nation's first black daily newspaper. Colleges that had long worked closely together took formal steps to organize the Atlanta University system in 1929, the year of Martin's birth.

Business and civic leaders — not simply avid golfers — made native son Bobby Jones the hero of the decade in 1930. He had won golf's "grand slam" — the U.S. Open, the U.S. Amateur, plus the British Open and Amateur titles.

Not even those closest to him imagined that a little black Atlantan, son of a pastor, would one day receive honors far beyond those bestowed upon Bobby Jones.

When Martin was three, economic problems of the Great Depression forced some governmental units to the wall. Fulton County, named for the Pennsylvania native who invented the

Atlanta tomb of assassinated civil rights leader

steamboat and set off from older DeKalb County under prodding
of Atlantan Edgar A. Angier — born in New Hampshire — was
relatively affluent. Atlanta's downtown business district kept the
county more than merely solvent.

Not so with adjoining Campbell and Milton counties. Facing
bankruptcy, they jumped at an opportunity to be annexed into
Fulton. When the two units, along with Cobb County's Roswell
district became part of Fulton County, it emerged as the state's
largest and most powerful.

Both Atlanta and Fulton County had unusual economic
strength that was fast increasing. Both also had big black communities. As a result — not foreseen in the 1930's — both Atlanta
and Fulton County eventually presented unusual if not unique
opportunities for development of black political and economic
leaders.

Young Martin probably gave such matters no thought; he
wanted to follow in the footsteps of the gentle man whom par-
ishioners revered as "Daddy King." He won a diploma from
Atlanta's Morehouse College, then received a theological degree
from Crozer Seminary before proceeding to Boston University.
When Boston conferred the Ph.D. degree upon him in 1955, he
was already regarded as both brilliant and highly individualistic.

Part of his individualism stemmed from the far-from-commonplace thinkers who greatly influenced him. Martin was attracted to the pacifism of Henry David Thoreau plus the philosophy of civil disobedience combined with nonviolence of Mahatma Gandhi. His mind was fired by exposure to the tenets of Walter Rausenbusch and the movement that liberal Protestantism termed the Social Gospel.

This was the man who accepted a call to become pastor of Dexter Avenue Baptist Church in Montgomery, Alabama. There, Rosa Parks' stubborn refusal to abide by time-honored patterns of racial segregation triggered the city's famous bus boycott. By the time that boycott was under way in December, 1955, the newly-arrived pastor had emerged as its leader.

Background and training plus unforeseen circumstances — combined with the intangible but powerful influence of knowing himself to be a black Martin Luther — propelled King into national prominence in the civil rights movement.

His goals were clearly specified very early. He wanted biracial cooperation coupled with abolition of "black codes" that severely limited black voting. Biracial cooperation plus the ballot would lead to his third and consuming goal, desegregation, the powerful orator assured audiences in many cities.

King's techniques seem deceptively simple, in retrospect. There was to be no violence, regardless of provocation. But blacks whom he persuaded and cajoled would stage marches, boycotts, sit-ins and every other conceivable form of peaceful protest.

America's black Martin Luther did not merely accept imprisonment as a consequence of his actions — he actively invited it. Jailed at least seventeen times, his 1963 "Letter from Birmingham Jail" was a classic denunciation of white moderates who elevated law and order above social justice.

Very early he saw that a cohesive organization was essential and consequently led in formation of the Southern Christian Leadership Conference. Growth of this movement was so rapid that King resigned his Alabama pastorate in order to become copastor with his father at Ebenezer Baptist Church, Atlanta. This gave him a base of operations as well as a salary while

Joseph Lowery

Mattiwilda Dobbs

permitting him to give practically full time to the SCLC and to the Student Nonviolent Coordinating Committee that it spawned.

When King was thirty-four he led the march on Washington and delivered his famous "I Have a Dream" speech. International recognition came with the award to him that year of the Nobel Peace Prize.

Yet, in the city of his birth, white economic and political leaders would have preferred to act as though the award meant little. Prodding by long-time Atlanta booster Ivan Allen, Jr., who was mayor in 1963, culminated in a huge interracial banquet — first of its sort in the city's history — honoring Martin Luther King, Jr.

Assassination of the black Martin Luther in Memphis in 1968 elevated him to the status of a martyr. There were racial riots in many cities but not in the city of his birth. Funeral services were held at Ebenezer Church, followed by a solemn procession — with a mule-drawn coffin — to Atlanta University and Morehouse College.

Strangely, King's struggle for social change — aided by colleagues and lieutenants such as Jesse Jackson, Andrew Young and Joseph Lowery — had its earliest and most dramatic success at the national level.

The Civil Rights Acts of 1964 and 1965 — bitterly denounced in most southern and many northern communities at the time — were seen as fruits of King's leadership. Establishment of the Atlantan's birthday as a national holiday, stubbornly resisted for years, cemented his place in history.

After a slow beginning, even the prophet of social change probably did not anticipate the rapidity with which his influence took effect in his home city. In 1960 he led about seventy-five demonstrators, mostly students, in a sit-in aimed at desegregation of food service at Rich's department store. Arrested, King was sent to notorious Reidsville Prison as a parole violator.

Barely a quarter-century later, Atlanta elected Maynard Jackson to serve as the city's first black mayor. Already half a dozen of the nation's top black business establishments were thriving here. Jackson's niece, Mattiwilda Dobbs, had gained renown as the first black to sing at famous La Scala opera house. White flight to suburbs, mostly northern, fostered black power in both the city of Atlanta and Fulton County.

Women were acknowledged to be second-class citizens until passage of the Nineteenth Amendment to the U.S. Constitution gave them theoretical equality at the polls. But it took half a century for that legislation to begin to achieve its full impact.

Blacks were fourth-class citizens even after legislation in the wake of Civil War gave them political equality with whites — on paper. It took a full century, culminating in the impassioned leadership and martyrdom of Martin Luther King, Jr., for changes envisioned by abolitionists of the nineteenth century to begin to take effect.

As much or more than any other Southern city, Atlanta had long before felt the full fury of Northern military might. From the city reborn from ashes of war came a black who, with his aides, permanently changed both the North and the South by effecting the most sweeping social reforms in American history.

Gone With The Wind

"Take it before I change my mind," Margaret Mitchell told a New York editor who said he wanted a look at her unfinished novel. Harold Latham bought a suitcase, stuffed the manuscript into it and caught a night train.

When Latham reached New Orleans, he found a telegram waiting for him at his hotel. "SEND IT BACK," the message began; "I'VE CHANGED MY MIND." It was too late; Latham had already made a decision to publish *Gone With the Wind*.

Margaret Mitchell and her novel are the stuff of which legends are made; authentic yarns about the woman and her story abound.

Harold Latham, vice-president of The Macmillan Company, had made several trips to Europe in search of new authors. Why not search in his own country? Once the question was raised, it seemed to answer itself. For no special reason, the editor chose Atlanta for an early scouting trip on this side of the Atlantic.

At the Atlanta Athletic Club, Latham met Peggy Mitchell — Mrs. John R. Marsh — and found her charming. His hostess told him, "If you're looking for a novel of the South, Peggy is your best bet."

Peggy overheard the comment and spoke up firmly: "I have no novel," she said, and turned the conversation to another topic.

World-famous novelist Margaret Mitchell

Latham later gave a detailed written account of events to editors of the *Atlanta Journal Magazine*.

Peggy Mitchell cheerfully agreed to show him some local sights — especially Druid Hills dogwoods in April and Stone Mountain. They talked in animated fashion about Southern literature. Yet every time Latham introduced the subject of his new friend's own work, she denied having produced the manuscript of a book. Preparing to leave the city that evening, he had a telephone call. Peggy Mitchell was in the downstairs lounge and wanted a word with him.

Latham went to the lounge and found "a tiny woman sitting on a divan, with the biggest manuscript beside her that I had ever seen, towering in two stacks almost to her shoulders." She explained that it was incomplete and unrevised but said he could take it if he wished.

"I hadn't any idea of letting you or any publisher see it," she explained. "I wrote it for my own entertainment."

Once in possession of the manuscript, the editor did buy a suitcase in which to pack it. He did start reading it on the train — headed to California by way of New Orleans. Scrupulously edited and given a carefully chosen title, it became *Gone With the Wind*. Earlier, *Tomorrow is Another Day* had been suggested and turned down — along with *Bugles Sang True* and *Tote the Weary Load*.

A sixth-generation Atlantan who spent her entire life in the city, Margaret Mitchell was a dropout from Smith College. According to her own account, she left college at the death of her mother and shortly afterward made her debut. She reported that she "ate chicken salad for a year, had a big time, and then got a job as a reporter on the *Atlanta Journal*."

"I married in 1925," she continued. "My husband is John R. Marsh, a former newspaperman but now manager of the advertising department of the Georgia Power Company. We have no children."

That first-person summary is significant, not so much for what it reveals as for what it conceals.

After a whirlwind courtship, she married Berrien K. Upshaw in September, 1922, a few weeks before her own twenty-second birthday. They reached a parting of the ways before the end of the

Reporter Peggy Mitchell at Georgia Tech, 1922

year, but their divorce was not granted until 1924.

While waiting for her divorce, Peggy became a staff member of the *Atlanta Journal Magazine,* sometimes writing feature articles for the daily newspaper as well. A very early assignment took her to the campus of Georgia Tech, where the petite reporter was photographed among towering athletes — apparently having the time of her life.

Not so, according to her own statements. She said that she found writing, "a fearful chore," and she once quipped that, "I'd rather pick cotton than write."

Stephens Mitchell, her brother, saw things differently.

He said that she began writing stories as soon as she learned to use a pencil — not even waiting to master spelling. She wrote for her own enjoyment, he insisted, originally using school tablets and storing penciled sheets in an enamel bread box.

If Stephens is to be believed rather than his famous sister, her own characterization of what she did best is a clue to her personality. *Gone With the Wind* is a fantasy that portrays a way of life that never existed — but in which Margaret Mitchell found escape and satisfaction.

Though it is beyond proof, there is strong support for the view according to which the fictional character she created, Scarlett

The movie version of occupied Atlanta

O'Hara, represents the person Peggy Mitchell most wanted to be.

Scarlett was conceived some time in 1926 when Peggy was recuperating from a broken ankle. After four years, she had given up her newspaper job due to what she described as "ill health, including a number of accidents, mostly automobile."

All accounts agree that she wrote the last chapter first — in order to stress a lesson imparted by her mother. Over and over, her mother had told the growing girl that survival, no matter what, is the key to life.

The impact of the Civil War upon a romanticized antebellum South provided an ideal vehicle for a novel whose theme was survival. Peggy Mitchell's head was crammed with war stories handed down to her by relatives.

In a rambling letter to a friend, she told him that chapters of her novel were not written in any sequence or order. Sometimes she rewrote a chapter a dozen times, put it away for a month, took it out for a fresh look — and then threw it away. Many chapters went through thirty revisions; one she reported to have been rewritten seventy times.

When published in 1936, the novel that editors had polished and arranged into a coherent whole did not win universal acclaim among critics. In the *New Republic,* it was characterized as "an

War-ravaged Tara, as depicted in GWTW

encyclopedia of the plantation legend." Members of the American Writers' Congress, voting for the year's best book, rejected the novel that for six years lay on closet shelves seldom touched and not submitted to a potential publisher.

If some critics were lukewarm, members of the general public were not. On a single day, bookstores reported sales in excess of fifty thousand copies. Within six months of publication the Atlanta woman's novel had topped the nation's previous all-time bestseller, *Uncle Tom's Cabin*.

Weeks before publication, signals from Hollywood indicated that there would be strong interest in a film version. Offered to MGM, it was turned down. Louis B. Mayer was guided by Irving Thalberg, who assured him that "No Civil War picture ever made a nickel."

David O. Selznick offered $50,000 for movie rights and as soon as a contract was signed let it be known that he intended to gamble. *Gone With the Wind* would be filmed entirely in color — the first full-length motion picture to be produced in such fashion.

Clark Gable didn't want the role of Rhett Butler but took it because he needed the money for a divorce. Nationwide publicity was generated by Selznick's search for "just the right woman to play Scarlett O'Hara" — whom Peggy Mitchell had initially called Pansy.

Illinois-born and Indiana-reared artist Wilbur G. Kurtz, an Atlantan by choice, had spent years preparing superb historical sketches and saving oral history about the Civil War. Since Margaret Mitchell flatly refused to have anything to do with the film version of her novel, the transplanted Yankee went to Hollywood as historical advisor for it.

Kurtz's insistence upon meticulous attention to detail resulted in some of the finest war scenes ever produced. Yet even he could not satisfy both producer and author on some all-important matters — notably the mansion known around the world as Tara.

Tara was not modeled after any existing plantation house, Margaret Mitchell said many times. Like the persons who were linked with it, Tara was wholly fictional. She envisioned it as a square house set on a hill, built of whitewashed brick and approached by an avenue of cedars.

Selznick's Tara, built on location, didn't remotely resemble the house as conceived by the author of the novel. That was one of the reasons Margaret Mitchell refused ever again to see the motion picture after its gala Atlanta premiere. Many devotees saw it twenty-five times or more; she scrupulously avoided the movie in which the drama of survival is far less obvious and compelling than in her novel.

A winner of ten Academy Awards, *Gone With the Wind* quickly propelled war-time Atlanta into world consciousness. Total box office receipts are estimated to be thirty to forty times the production cost of just over $4 million. Surpassed by other movies in gross receipts only in recent years, Margaret Mitchell's story would perhaps remain the all-time Hollywood financial triumph if earnings were adjusted for inflation.

Its accident-prone creator, who launched the project for her own entertainment during a period of recuperation from a broken bone, was killed by a taxicab when crossing an Atlanta street.

From the day of its publication until her death in 1949, Mitchell was almost totally absorbed with her book — faithfully edited to conform with her own concepts. Repudiating the movie version, she may have been most satisfied with its final line.

Selznick shot two versions of Rhett's walking out on Scarlett but violently opposed using "Frankly, dear, I just don't care." Eventually he paid a $5,000 fine in order to use the ending of his choice: "Frankly, my dear, I don't give a damn."

"Forward Atlanta" — Branch-Office Town To Home-Office Center

"This place is great! I'm going to stay!"

That decision on the part of a nineteen-year-old visitor to Atlanta's Cotton Expo of 1895 was of interest only to Ivan Allen and his family. Born in Dalton, Georgia, he had doubted that he would like the larger city — but changed his mind within twenty-four hours of reaching it.

Already a crack salesman of typewriters, he had no trouble finding work. Eventually he became a partner in the firm, then built it into the Ivan Allen Company. Repudiating the then-accepted specialty approach adopted by office-supply firms, Allen devised a "department store" concept that was new in the field. It brought quick and lasting success.

By 1925 when Allen had been in Atlanta for thirty years, his adopted city faced a new crisis. This time, trouble centered in the South rather than in the North. Booming Florida was luring long-established Atlantans to Tampa and Miami — and was getting new establishments that earlier would have come to Atlanta.

Business and civic leaders made plans to launch a national advertising program with a then-stupendous budget of $850,000 over three years. To head the Forward Atlanta program, backers turned to Allen. His business success plus his always exuberant enthusiasm about Atlanta made him a natural choice for the post.

Allen plastered the nation with praise of the city's climate, altitude, labor supply, low cost of living, educational and medical facilities. A 1929 summary indicated that Forward Atlanta had brought 762 new establishments with twenty thousand employees and annual payrolls of more than $34 million.

Ivan Allen, Jr.

Many of the newcomers were branch-office operations of nationally prominent firms. So many located in Allen's adopted home that Atlanta became known everywhere as "a great little branch-office town."

For Ivan Allen, his son and namesake, Ivan Allen, Jr., and others like them, that was good — but not good enough. Before the end of the Great Depression, key Atlantans were dreaming of the day when their city would be recognized as a booming home-office center. Frequent campaigns directed toward that goal — one of them still in progress — helped executives to reach decisions to come to Atlanta.

C. E. Woolman

One such person was Indiana native C. E. Woolman, who came South to help fight the boll weevil. At Louisiana State University, he developed a radical new plan: using airplanes to dust cotton and other crops with insect poison.

Federal officials listened with interest, then provided two Army-owned DeHavilland DN-4's for field tests. They were so successful that a New York plane builder put Woolman at the head of a new division — the Huff Daland.

Huff Daland sent twelve pilots, fifteen mechanics and eighteen specially equipped planes to Macon, Georgia, in the year that

Crop duster from which Delta Air Lines was born

Forward Atlanta was conceived. They gave middle Georgia farmers five dustings for seven dollars an acre but found fields too small for commercial success in the new venture.

Woolman sent planes and crews to try their luck in immense valleys of Peru. There they made money and triggered for Woolman a spinoff idea. Why not use planes to transport mail great distances over rugged terrain?

Against stiff German competition, he won a franchise that made his company the first airline operator south of the equator in the Western Hemisphere. Then Woolman found financial backing with which to buy all Huff Daland equipment. It formed the operating fleet of a new corporation named for the Mississippi delta where the home office was located. Newly formed Delta Air Service continued to dust crops but expected quickly to move into air mail and passenger service.

After having expanded many times, Delta moved its headquarters to Atlanta in 1941 to take advantage of the fast-developing municipal airport. One of the earliest top-level corporations to choose Atlanta for its home office, Delta now employs about twelve thousand persons in the city and twice as many elsewhere.

South American experience helped Delta to lead the way in development of international routes from Atlanta, capped in 1986

by the launching of direct flights to
Tokyo, a route coveted by com-
petitors. Annually, Delta enplane-
ments at Hartsfield International have
hovered close to 50 percent of the
field's total.

Owen Cheatham

Selection of Marietta as the home
of Lockheed-Georgia, an outgrowth
of Bell Aircraft, also in the Cobb
County region of metro Atlanta,
meant local industry that is big in
every sense of the term.
Production of the C-130 Hercules
propjet transport began in 1954. Less than a decade later the
Japanese Air Self-Defense Force received Hercules number seventeen hundred. Today Lockheed-Georgia is producing the
world's biggest transport planes.

Atlanta's skyline gains part of its distinctiveness from the pink
marble exterior and unique architecture of the tallest office building in the Southeast. It is here because the Georgia-Pacific Corporation, a giant in the forest industry, elected in 1982 to leave
Portland, Oregon, in favor of the city Ivan Allen helped to boost
toward a new role as home-office center.

Virginia native Owen R. Cheatham launched the business in
Augusta, Georgia, during the second year of the Forward Atlanta
campaign. With personal savings and $6,000 in borrowed money,
he bought a lumber yard and initially ran it in conventional
fashion.

Cheatham soon began a program of diversification that is still
in progress. T. Marshall Hahn oversees the $6.7 billion per year
business from his office on the fifty-first floor of that downtown
Atlanta building that no one ever forgets, once having seen it.

With more than thirty-eight thousand persons on the payroll,
Georgia-Pacific owns 4.7 million acres of North American tim-
berlands and controls another 480,000 acres. Long a leader in
production of soft plywood, the company turns out more than
four billion square feet annually. Though less spectacular, production of paper, corrugated packaging and tissue products is

Lockheed's 1,700th Hercules propjet transport

measured in millions of tons. Hahn's announced goal is to push G-P's paper business to the level of its huge building products segment.

While her skyline has been undergoing dramatic change, other aspects of Atlanta have not remained static.

Ivan Allen, Jr., not only took over the family business but also adopted his father's passionate desire to see the city move forward. As 1947 head of the Community Chest fund drive, he faced a personal dilemma. A business executive had invited him to attend a dinner launching the drive in the black community. Should he observe accepted standards and decline — or risk white wrath by accepting.

When the thirty-six-year-old future mayor of Atlanta consulted his father, Ivan Allen, Sr., spoke bluntly. Persons of his generation had failed to solve the most important issue confronting them, he said. That issue was racial justice — without which no number of home offices would bring Atlanta to the level of genuine greatness.

Ivan Allen, Jr., broke with tradition and went to the Community Chest dinner. Later as mayor, he persuaded many fearful and angry whites that their own welfare, as well as that of Atlanta, required a new outlook and fresh patterns of conduct —

regardless of how some personally despised Martin Luther King, Jr., and the goals for which he stood.

If he were alive, Ivan Allen, Sr., would swing his fancy cane and tip his pearl-gray fedora that was his trademark. Then he'd note that the city from which the Coca-Cola Company and scores of newcomers emerged has not experienced the racial violence of Chicago, Los Angeles, Boston and other cities. Underscoring Atlanta's achievements and delighting in them, Allen would doubtless urge acceleration of forward movement on many fronts.

A Terrorist Bomb
That Backfires

"When the wolves of hate are loosed on one people, then no one is safe."

Taken from context and standing alone, that verdict seems almost commonplace. Who with a grain of decency and common sense would debate it?

Deciphered from badly scratched microfilm and viewed as a tiny segment of a truly explosive page-one editorial in the *Atlanta Constitution,* Ralph McGill's sentence becomes pregnant with meaning.

Monday, October 13, 1958, saw the entire front page of the newspaper devoted to a single story and reaction to events detailed in that story.

Before daylight on Sunday (a day clearly selected for the deed) hatemongers were at work. Their dynamite bomb blasted a gaping hole in the wall of the Atlanta Temple on Peachtree Street. Terrorists fled in the dark.

Jack Tarver, president of the *Atlanta Journal and Constitution,* offered a $5,000 reward for arrest and conviction "or the committal to a suitable mental institution of the feeble-minded morons responsible."

That reward was never paid.

Months of police work led to indict-
ment of five members of the National
States Rights Party. Two trials were
held despite scanty physical evidence
— much of it destroyed by the blast.
One court session ended in a mistrial,
the second in an acquittal.

Ralph McGill

Yet time showed that the bomb had
backfired.

Ralph McGill's full-column editorial brought him the 1959 Pulitzer
Prize for editorial writing. More
important, it served as a catalyst to
activate thousands in the city and surrounding regions who
deplored anti-Jewish activity but seldom did anything to try to
stop it.

Decades earlier the lynching of business executive Leo Frank
had been condoned by high-ranking officials of the state. Increasing talk in Washington pointed to the likelihood of legislation
aimed at protection of rights of minorities. In the climate of
widespread opposition to work of Martin Luther King and his
followers, hatemongers turned against Jews as well as against
blacks.

Dynamite that ripped a beautiful place of worship in Atlanta,
McGill pointed out, had come "hard on the heels of a like
destruction of a handsome high school at Clinton, Tennessee.

"The same rabid, mad-dog minds were without question
behind both. The school house and the church are the targets of
diseased, hate-filled minds.

"Let us face the facts. This is a harvest. It is the crop of things
sown. It is the harvest of defiance of courts and the encouragement of citizens to defy law on the part of many Southern
politicians.

"This, too, is a harvest of those so-called Christian ministers
who have chosen to preach hate instead of compassion. You do
not preach and encourage hatred for the Negro and hope to
restrict it to that field. When the wolves of hate are loosed on one
people, then no one is safe.

"For a long time now it has been needed for all Americans to stand up and be counted on the side of law and the due process of law — even when it goes against personal beliefs and emotions. But there is yet time."

Many decent, law-abiding white Christians were initially distressed by McGill's editorial. Some were outraged. Taken at face value, the sermon by a man who had joined the *Atlanta Constitution* as a sportswriter three decades earlier meant that goals and values must be reappraised. No number of best-selling novels and booming corporations would make Atlanta a good place to live, so long as Jews or blacks or any other group of persons were subject to legalized oppression or wanton attack.

Second and third readings of the prize-winning editorial, linked with formal and informal discussion of it, led great numbers of persons to see things a bit differently. Gradually it became clear that in his anger and indignation, McGill had spoken for silent multitudes of Atlantans and Southerners in general. Though not actively working for change, a strong minority of citizens — perhaps even a slim majority — were already sick at their stomachs over endless bickering and strife about race, religion, rights of women and other social issues.

"It is late. But there is still time," said McGill in a combined warning-promise issued ninety-seven years after a devastated nation ended its most deadly war. Other voices took up the editor's refrain — so many that, in the end, the bomb that leveled a house of worship backfired upon the terrorists who used it.

Few metropolitan centers in the nation or anywhere else in the world have a better climate of tolerance and mutual respect across social boundaries than does Atlanta today. That climate will prevail and improve — so long as all citizens remember McGill's warning: "When the wolves of hate are loosed on one people, then no one is safe."

Borglum's head of Robert E. Lee — blasted off in 1926

Centerpiece of today's Stone Mountain Park

Heroes Of The Lost Cause Loom Far Larger Than In Life

A Michelangelo, it is not. But the world's biggest sculpture, carved by techniques unknown to medieval masters, would cause the artist's eyes to open wide with wonder. What's more, the enduring stuff of which the sculpture is made practically guarantees that it will be around when art treasures of Europe exist only as dim memories.

For nearly two hundred years, visitors from afar have been awestruck by the immensity of the mass of granite that made the sculpture possible. At least as early as 1790 an occasional white man, guided by Creek Indians, climbed the monolith that came to be called Rock Mountain.

John T. Graves of New York encountered the mountain much later, in 1912. He was so stirred by it that he wrote for his *New York American* newspaper an editorial. It challenged artisans to create man's biggest work of art on what he called "the world's finest piece of stone."

Unveiled in 1972 after decades of effort, the Stone Mountain Memorial may not be exactly what Yankee Graves had in mind. For members of the Atlanta chapter, United Daughters of the Confederacy, saw a unique opportunity there and acted upon it. As a result, the world's biggest carving commemorates Confederate leaders.

New Gibraltar in 1849, with train at flag stop

Erect on their immense granite steeds, Jefferson Davis and Robert E. Lee and Stonewall Jackson look as though they plan to ride on forever.

They should; backers of the plan to create a lasting memorial found that execution of the idea seemed to take forever.

Noted sculptor Gutzon Borglum completed designs and started carving in 1923. After six months, on Lee's birthday, the general's partly-finished head was unveiled before Mayor Jimmy Walker of New York City and twenty thousand others.

Borglum was famous for temper tantrums. One hit him in 1925. He destroyed every model and sketch he had made. That left the UDC holding short-term title to a work of art barely started.

Augustus Lukeman scrapped Borglum's master plan, blasted off work in progress, and used jackhammers to fashion a panel 305 feet wide, 190 feet high. He managed to finish two faces and to outline Lee's famous horse, Traveller. When a suitable monument was not completed by March 20, 1928, owners who had given a conditional deed to the mountain reclaimed it.

Another twenty years passed. Then the Georgia Legislature bought 3,200 acres that included the biggest exposed hunk of solid granite in the known universe. Before anyone envisioned

Precarious visit to carving-in-progress, about 1928

that New Gibraltar, as it was known then, would be included in metro Atlanta, it had been a flag stop on the Georgia Railroad. A century later, lawmakers hoped it would become a stopping point for Florida-bound tourists.

Walter K. Hancock of Massachusetts — another Yankee — won in nationwide competition for the job of completing what Borglum and Lukeman had started. Hancock licked the mountain. Under his direction, workmen used a thermo-jet torch to chip it off a fragment at a time until three immense figures emerged. Robert E. Lee, as seen today, bears little resemblance to the Lee of Borglum or Lukeman. There is no truth, however, to the widely-circulated story that Lee's steed was initially given ears of a mule rather than a horse.

Open every day, the park that has developed around the mountain is a top tourist attraction of the Southeast. Annually it attracts more than six million visitors. Some who come from foreign countries have never heard of the Confederate States of America until they reach the mountain.

No one who is overpowered by the biggest of all carvings will ever forget that "The Lost Cause" had heroes whose mythologized figures loom much larger than in life.

Clustered around the 583-acre monolith that is Stone Mountain is a complex of nineteen restored and furnished antebellum buildings. There's also a 363-acre lake — complete with paddlewheel boats — and a rail line with replicas of Civil War trains.

Golf, tennis, fishing, an auto and music museum, a skating trail and a 732-bell electronic carillon probably wouldn't have developed where they are, had there been no gigantic carving.

Granite from the rock table upon which the mountain sits can be seen at several MARTA stations — most vividly, perhaps, at Peachtree Center. Oglethorpe University's first-of-a-kind time capsule is buried in that same stratum. Colonel Marinus Willet, a leader of the Sons of Liberty during the American Revolution and one of the first persons to describe the mountain in writing, had no idea that the monolith is merely a "bubble" on the surface of an unimaginably vast layer of granite.

Owned and operated by the State of Georgia, the park that includes the mountain and its unequalled carving is completely self-supporting. Somewhat strangely in an era when even small projects in the arts often seek and get federal aid, the world-champion carving didn't receive from Washington a grant of even one red cent.

Davis, Lee and Jackson would approve.

After 1860, they had no use for anything federal.

State-Of-The-Art Transit System Due To 461 Voters

Completion of the long-delayed Confederate Memorial at Stone Mountain came during an era of rapid change on many fronts.

Andrew Young became the first Southern black to go to Congress since the Reconstruction era. Now the nation's twentieth-largest city, Atlanta was calling itself "The Hub of the South" — symbolic of her transition from state capital and significant city to dominant metropolis of the eastern sunbelt, north of Miami.

During eight years as mayor, Ivan Allen, Jr., had taken giant steps to unify a city whose one-half million citizens were fifty-one percent black. Allen personally negotiated a compromise during racial sit-ins. He integrated the cafeteria at City Hall and hired blacks for significant posts. In spite of violent opposition from many constituents and peers, Atlanta's mayor supported the 1964 Civil Rights Act in testimony before Congress.

Two vital steps had to be taken, said the man who exemplified the spirit of "Forward Atlanta," before genuine greatness could be achieved. There simply had to be a metro rapid transit system and a municipal stadium.

Georgia voters gave approval to the state constitution's amendment in 1964. Under terms of the revision, a regional unified transit system could be established to serve Fulton, DeKalb, Cobb, Gwinnett and Clayton Counties.

Opposition was instant, violent and widespread. Fulton and DeKalb voters rejected a 1968 plan by which a start could be made from sale of bonds backed by property taxes. Metropolitan Atlanta Rapid Transit Authority, or MARTA, existed as a paper agency only. There were no funds with which to build.

Rawson Haverty, Sr., was persuaded to head a committee of one hundred volunteers. Their goal: creation of grass-roots support for the proposed system.

Sam Massell, the city's first Jewish mayor, had gained the office at age forty-two — just a decade after Ralph McGill had urged, wheedled, cajoled and threatened citizens who backed the bombing of a Temple or any similar act. It was Massell who came up with a radical new idea: ask voters to pay an additional sales tax of one cent for a period of ten years in order to get MARTA off the drawing boards.

Black insurance executive Jesse Hill became an articulate and persuasive backer of the revised funding plan. Along with volunteers from Haverty's committee, he tried to convince voters — both black and white — that their own self-interest was deeply involved.

As November, 1971, approached, everyone agreed that the referendum was in deep trouble. Sentiment in outlying counties was almost solidly against any form of taxation or any type of participation in a metro system. Though approval in Fulton and DeKalb could bring MARTA into functional existence, fate of the issue was in doubt even in these central counties.

Numerous industries and business establishments took out display advertisements urging voters to say "Yes." All eight of Rich's stores remained closed until 10:30 A.M. on November 9, in order to encourage both employees and customers to go to the polls early.

As expected, few voters of outlying counties favored the plan. DeKalb endorsed it by a healthy margin — and all-important Fulton hung in the balance. A preliminary count showed approval in that county by a margin of 2,011 votes.

Proponents of MARTA rejoiced; opponents demanded and got

Rapid transit train over interstate highways

Marta's Five Points Station

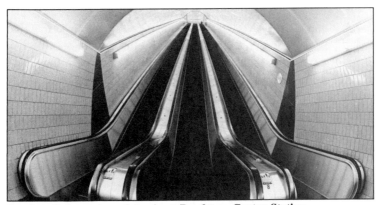

Southeast's longest escalator is at Peachtree Center Station

a recount. This time, the tally showed that precisely 461 voters —
some of them having used absentee ballots — had put the referendum over the top. Governor Jimmy Carter presented to Mayor
Massell the pen with which he signed the transit legislation.

Directors of the transit system reported assets of $2.2 billion on
June 30, 1985. Which means that those 461 voters whose "Yes"
made MARTA a reality had infinitely more impact than they
thought. Operating revenue aside, each vote was worth more than
$4.7 million.

This was not dimly realized at the time. Neither did anyone —
Massell, Haverty, Hill, Richard Rich or any other enthusiastic
proponent of MARTA — realize how all-important the timing
was.

Huge amounts of federal money, along with absolutely essential revenue from the sales tax, enabled planners to seek — and to
get — the best. Starting from scratch rather than upgrading an
antiquated system, MARTA's builders could and did take advantage of the finest of space-age technology.

Many other cities have patchwork systems — partly new,
partly very old. Numerous other metro areas tried to get into the
federal money chest too late, when immense sums were no longer
available from Washington.

Had voters approved a MARTA system half a century earlier, it
would have been obsolete before completion. Had they deferred
their approval another twenty years, funding would have been
impossible.

After voters approved the rapid transit system but before major
construction got under way, the city went through another period
of trauma. Sam Massell was defeated for reelection in the aftermath of a bitter contest that brought racial tension to a level many
hoped they would never again see.

Mayor Maynard Jackson, first black to hold the office, was
forced to face a dwindling tax base and fast-increasing traffic
problems. Expansion of the interstate highway system plus growth
of MARTA greatly reduced congestion in the streets. Despite a
high vacancy rate in commercial space, big-ticket high-rise buildings continue to go up—boosting the tax base.

Mayor Andrew Young subsequently succeeded in healing

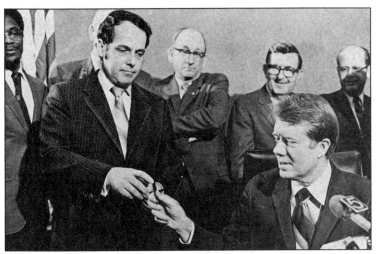

Gov. Jimmy Carter presents pen to Mayor Sam Massell

many old wounds. Atlanta is solidly black in terms of its political base, and Fulton County is heavily so. But Young's personal charisma in combination with his established international reputation enabled him to keep the respect and the support of the white establishment as well.

In this climate, the growth rate of the city is the most rapid in its history. Home offices of corporations are built and branch offices are established at a rate that continues to climb. More and more of them are coming from Britain, Europe, Asia, Africa and South America.

Few if any decisions to come to Atlanta are based solely on the fact that no other city has a transit system that can rival MARTA. But even most who initially opposed its creation now agree that MARTA is a vital ingredient in the present health and continuing expansion of the metro area.

Hank Aaron hammers his record-breaking 715th homer

Hank Aaron Makes Baseball History

As Hank Aaron moved toward the plate, 53,775 spectators jumped to their feet, screaming. Photographers surged forward, cameras at the ready. With Al Downing of the Dodgers on the mound, everyone in the Atlanta-Fulton County stadium knew that this could be the moment.

Henry ("The Hammer") Aaron had launched his baseball career twenty-two years earlier in Eau Claire, Wisconsin. Fans began to go wild when the player for the Atlanta Braves hammered his 710th home run. Babe Ruth's record was sure to fall — but when and where?

Ruth, long the subject of national adulation as "The King of Swat," drove in his own last homer — No. 714 — as a member of the Braves, then centered in Boston. Unbroken for thirty-seven years, his record was about to be shattered.

Aaron badly wanted to supplant Ruth in the record books in a home game. With his tying homer already recorded, he racked up No. 715 on April 8, 1974, in Atlanta. Hence, it is appropriate that the stadium in which that hit was made includes a life-size bronze statue of Aaron that was executed by noted sculptor Ed Dwight of Denver.

"The Hammer" went on to hit another forty homers, retired

from play and became vice-president and director of player development for the Braves.

He's the first to acknowledge that he couldn't have succeeded in breaking Babe Ruth's record precisely as he did had it not been for Atlanta's Ivan Allen, Jr.

Civic leader and booster Allen, whose father had set him a superb example, saw the need for a municipal stadium as second only to that for a mass transit system. When he retired from office as Atlanta's chief executive, MARTA was still an unrealized dream waiting for voter endorsement.

Mayor Allen didn't wait for taxpayers to give their approval before launching work on a stadium, however. Preliminary talks had indicated that baseball's Athletics, then in Kansas City, would look favorably upon an opportunity to move to Atlanta. But in order to do so, they'd have to have a place in which to play.

Allen went to Mills B. Lane of C&S Bank and got his pledge to provide the money with which to put a long-dormant Stadium Authority to work. They chose a site not far from Hartsfield International, near three interstate highways, and gave architects the go-ahead. National publicity generated by big league baseball would give Atlanta another big boost, Mayor Allen said.

Negotiations with the Kansas City franchise owners fell through — with the Atlanta-Fulton County stadium already under construction. Owners of the Milwaukee Braves, believed to be in a financial squeeze, came to Atlanta for discussions with Allen, Lane and key leaders of the business community. They agreed to sell. However, before the move could be made, the new stadium was ready for use.

Elevated to Triple-A status only a short time earlier, the old Atlanta Crackers played their last baseball game in the city — and first in the new stadium — at the tail end of the 1965 season.

The Atlanta Braves opened the 1966 season in April in their new home. Five months later the Atlanta Falcons took to the gridiron under a new franchise that permitted the NFL to expand to the city.

No other city has entered the ranks of big league baseball plus big league football in a single year. Completion of the Omni, a sixteen thousand-seat downtown stadium built by utilizing air

Bobby Jones (left) shares British Open trophy with fellow Atlantans

rights over the railroad gulch that shaped early Atlanta, gave basketball new prominence. The Atlanta Hawks meet opponents there — and the availability of MARTA transportation has made the Omni a favorite site for regional play-offs.

By 1986, fans were saying that existing facilities were far too small. Falcons owner Rankin Smith, Sr., responded by saying that his family would finance a seventy thousand-seat domed stadium for football — at no risk to taxpayers. Concurrently, analysts recommended building a state-of-the-art baseball stadium of forty-five thousand seats to be ready for use by the Atlanta Braves no later than 1995.

Mayor Allen made the Forward Atlanta program, first led by his father, a permanent feature of the city's life. He rejoiced at the coming of big-league sports and frequent use of "Atlanta" in news coverage of games.

Decades earlier, all-time golf great Bobby Jones and clay court tennis champion Bitsy Grant had made the name of the city familiar to persons who never before heard of it. Though they were not Atlantans, Ty Cobb and Jackie Robinson of Georgia had boosted the image of the state's capital. Now the Braves, the Falcons and the Hawks would do infinitely more than had individual sports heroes!

Far-sighted as he was, even the mayor who often elevated the city's priorities above his personal concerns probably didn't anticipate a wedding between big-league sports and hi-tech communications. Ohio-born R. E. ("Ted") Turner saw what such a match would mean. He bought control of the Braves in 1976, thereby gaining a big "plus" for his expanding commu-

R. E. "Ted" Turner

nications empire. Plugged on TV as "America's team," the Braves have won devoted followers who habitually watch action from a distance but who come to Atlanta for games at intervals.

Partly because more and more TV makes more and more sports coverage profitable, Turner took a big gamble by launching — and covering — the international Goodwill Games in Moscow in 1986. Long-range impact of these games cannot be assessed until more have been held. Regardless of how they affect Turner's TV enterprises, multitudes of viewers in faraway places will have learned that they were launched by an entrepreneur from Atlanta, in the state of Georgia, U.S.A.

Had Hank Aaron ended his career with a 714th homer — or had he driven his 715th into the bleachers in a distant stadium — the story of big league sports in Atlanta, plus TV involvement in it, might have been quite different.

High Museum Commemorates Woman Who First Gave Art A Home

Honor after honor, plus still-growing international recognition, has come to Atlanta's High Museum of Art since construction of a permanent home — an eye-catching building designed by Richard Meier.

Only old-timers in the city remember that the institution's name has no connection with a "lofty" structure or an "elevated" list of exhibits. Mrs. J. M. High wanted and got that name as a living memorial to her dead husband. She didn't anticipate that she, too, would be commemorated.

Eight women incorporated the Atlanta Art Association in 1905 with the goal of promoting interest in the arts and establishing a museum and an art school. It took half a century for their organization to get its first building designed for such use.

Earlier, though, the residence of Mrs. J. M. High and daughters became the High Museum of Art. Born at Sandtown plantation on the Chattahoochee River, Harriet Wilson — Hattie, to relatives and friends — married Madison, Georgia, native Joseph M. High at age nineteen in 1882.

High had come to Atlanta in 1880 to operate a dry goods store in partnership with E. D. Herring. Within two years of having taken over the establishment at No. 48 Whitehall Street, High had

Rodin's "The Shade" was a gift from France

pushed it into ranks of the city's "big five" retail stores.
At the death of her husband, Hattie High became one of the
South's earliest female executives. She ran the store for fifteen
years and watched it grow steadily. She then sold out — but
stipulated that her husband's name be retained by the new owners.
Hattie's Greek Revival girlhood home had symbolized affluence. Sherman and his men changed that. Her father having died,
the girl and her mother came to Atlanta. In the growing town of
twenty thousand, Mrs. Wilson operated a boarding house and
took in sewing.

Her daughter's marriage to High brought prosperity and a
return to affluence. Hattie went to Europe most years and spent
one entire winter in Paris. She established a fund for research and
purchase of books at the municipal library. In England, she
located fine oil portraits of General and Lady James Oglethorpe
and presented them to the Atlanta university that commemorates
Georgia's founder. She contributed to the Berry School in the
mountains of north Georgia and gave both time and money to
North Avenue Presbyterian Church.

Still, Atlantans were stunned by the 1926 news that Hattie High
had given her Tudor-style mansion at Peachtree and 15th Streets to
the Atlanta Art Association.

As a girl, she had studied art — a little, at least — as a student
at Mrs. Josephine Ballard's private school. She had sketched and
painted as a hobby, but even after becoming wealthy she had
shown no interest in collecting works of art.

Yet her mansion and its grounds proved strangely suitable for
display of paintings and works of sculpture. For a generation after
her 1932 death, her former residence was the primary building of
the Art Association. A new structure was erected for it in 1955;
eight years later, the residence was demolished.

Voters rejected a 1962 plan to create an arts center in Piedmont
Park. That June, 106 Atlanta art patrons returning from a
museum-sponsored European tour were killed in a plane crash at
Orly Field, Paris. Grief-stricken France sent a gift of a replica of a
famous Rodin statue; as a memorial to victims, Atlantans erected
a new and larger arts center in 1968.

Today that building houses the Atlanta Symphony Orchestra,

Interior ramps, High Museum of Art

Alliance Theater and Atlanta College of Art. All of them are basic components of the Woodruff Art Center.

Nearby, the gleaming new $20 million High Museum of Art came into existence as a result of big challenge gifts. Robert W. Woodruff channeled Coca-Cola money into the center, which received major support from the Callaway Foundation as well. Thousands of smaller gifts completed the necessary funding.

In its permanent collection the museum includes more than seven thousand works of art. The 135,000-square-foot facility has ample space for even "blockbuster" traveling shows.

New York, Chicago, St. Louis and other American cities have older and larger art collections that delight both residents and visitors. Yet Atlanta remains in a class all by itself. It was not a transportation magnate of the Vanderbilt genre or an industrial tycoon like Carnegie who realized that a city cannot live upon dry goods emporia and hotels and railroads alone.

Thanks to a widow with vision, only Atlanta has a museum of art that was launched in the former residence of a merchant.

Georgia Tech Suits Up
For Century Two

Cotton was king. "Hi-tech," a shorthand label for computer-age technology, wouldn't be coined for decades. Mules were the nation's most common sources of energy in 1882, and steam locomotives were the most sophisticated. China seemed almost as distant as the moon. Anyone who babbled about some day putting men into space would have been a sure-fire candidate for a mental institution.

It was in that climate that Confederate veterans Nathaniel E. Harris and J. F. Hanson began crusading for establishment of a technical school in Georgia. Lawmakers appropriated $65,000 in 1885, then asked interested cities to bid for the proposed school.

Five offers of land, buildings and money were received. Most came from old, established centers. Atlanta, still regarded as a brash upstart, promised $70,000 plus four acres of land and $2,500 a year for operations. That brought the coveted school to the city — whose gratis land was located on the far side of a huge gully. When the first building went up, a foot bridge was erected so students could get into Atlanta from "their isolated fortress with its dry moat."

Nominally a unit of the University of Georgia, the new institution had its own board of trustees and president from the start.

Georgia School (now Institute) of Technology, 1890

Full autonomy came in 1932 when the University System of Georgia was created.

Since the start of classes in 1888, Tech's campus has grown to more than 320 acres. Once on the outskirts — "far from beautiful Peachtree and busy Marietta" — it has become a hi-tech island in midtown.

Money from the north — Pittsburgh, no less — launched a textile department when Tech was just nine years old. Today the school has the only fully accredited school of textiles in the nation.

With aerospace engineering growing rapidly in importance, there has been a wedding between disciplines. Flexible joints for astronauts' suits were developed at Tech, where research continues at full speed.

Writing in "Hi-Tech Atlanta," Dick Gentry noted the dramatic shift in the atmosphere on campus, once noted for winning football teams, entertainment of presidents and other visiting celebrities, and throwing of elegant parties. "Cinderella has changed," he says. "Those glass slippers are gone and the new ones are all silicon. Prince Charming is so busy working on his doctorate that the balls aren't fun any more."

Real action during Tech's second century is likely to be in micro-electronics laboratories, development of guidance systems for tactical missiles, and information storage and exchange of mind-blowing speed and capacity. A strong and growing "Chinese connection" has brought an increasing two-way flow of instructors and students between Atlanta and mainland China. Tech helped to bring the 1996 Summer Olympics to the city, and began building for The Games in 1990.

With her 12,000-student enrollment growing, the school that was launched with the hope it could boost agriculture in Georgia is a key center of research for the nation's Strategic Defense Initiative, or "Star Wars." Now about equally divided between males and females, about ten percent of the long-time all-male student body is made up of men and women from seventy-six foreign countries that range from Nepal to Zimbabwe. Asia provides about one foreign student in ten.

Because of Tech's presence, at least a dozen hi-tech enterprises are expected to form annually in Atlanta or relocate from other regions. Yet the biggest enterprise spawned by Tech is neither commercial nor hi-tech.

Before World War I, administrators decided that growing Atlanta needed to offer more educational opportunities to persons who flocked to the city without waiting to earn college degrees. As a result, an Evening School of Commerce — designed for working males and females — was launched in 1913.

Three years later, the Tech offspring graduated its first seven students.

Fifty years afterward, the offspring has become Georgia State University — nearly three times as large as the parent institution and exceeded in enrollment among regional institutions only slightly by the University of Georgia in Athens.

Unlike Emory, Oglethorpe, Mercer and Agnes Scott College, G.S.U. is solidly downtown — within easy walking distance of Five Points. Instead of spreading outward, campus growth has been upward. Students — still heavily weighted toward persons with full-time jobs — converge upon high-rise buildings not

Georgia State University, as approached from Five Points

distinctly different from nearby office towers.

In the metro area, however, only G.S.U. students can register in a different fashion — by telephone.

As an urban life center, the downtown university is in high national esteem. Education, one of its six colleges, includes a one-of-a-kind child development center that has had much media attention. With a faculty of two hundred, the College of Business is rated a bit below Duke and Emory by academicians. But it turns out more M.B.A.'s than does either university. Third largest teacher education institution in the nation, G.S.U. is the biggest in the Southeast.

Aware of approximately equivalent job opportunities in two or more cities, increasing numbers of young adults choose Atlanta in order to pursue a Georgia State University education, before or after working hours.

Doc Pemberton's Secret Formula

Pharmacist John S. Pemberton, a cavalry captain during the Civil War, believed Atlanta was an up and coming town. Doc, as he was universally known, decided to take his business to the rail center instead of returning to staid, old and aristocratic Columbus, Georgia.

Railroad workers, drummers and persons arriving from elsewhere, as well as old-timers in Atlanta, liked Pemberton and his wares: Indian Queen Hair Dye, Globe of Flower Cough Syrup, Triplex Liver Pills and French Wine Coca. Especially the last — touted as "a Delightful Nerve Tonic and Stimulant that Never Intoxicates."

Because brash, young Atlanta was not nearly so predictable as older and more staid communities, Doc Pemberton kept his ear to the ground. Rumblings he picked up in the summer of 1885 disturbed him, but plenty. He'd just completed a new chemical plant at a cost of $160,000; now there were rumors that Fulton County voters would go for local-option prohibition.

Rumors proved correct. When votes were counted after the November referendum, the county — and the town that served as its center — went bone dry by a margin of 228 votes.

By the time saloons closed on July 1, 1886, Doc Pemberton

was ready. Reputedly using a three-
legged iron pot in the back yard of his
residence, he concocted a new formula to replace outlawed French Wine
Coca. Capitalizing upon exotic ingre-
dients — coca from South America
and kola from Africa — he called the
new mixture Coca-Cola.

Despite its name, the product mar-
keted as "the Ideal Brain Tonic" and
reliever of fatigue didn't win many
devotees. During a twelve-month
period, Pemberton spent $73.96 on

"Doc" Pemberton

advertising in order to sell twenty-five one-gallon kegs at two
dollars each. That's why word got out that he was about ready to
sell his formula.

One person interested in it was another wholesale druggist.
Asa G. Candler had spent three years as apprentice to physicians
in Cartersville, Georgia. He struck out for Atlanta with a single
dollar plus a few small coins in his pocket but soon managed to
begin producing and selling patent medicines.

Candler bought a fractional interest in Coca-Cola, then other
portions of the formula. In a series of complicated purchases that
ended in 1891, he wound up as sole owner — with an investment
in the Pemberton mixture of $2,300. Had voters not briefly
outlawed alcohol, there's no reason to believe that Coca-Cola
would have been created.

Early newspaper ads by Candler devoted equal space to his new
nerve tonic and to Delactalave — billed as "The Great Tooth-
wash." Despite Candler's business acumen, Coca-Cola might
never have gotten past the patent-medicine phase had not two
developments taken place spontaneously — even accidentally.

At Jacobs' Pharmacy, corner of Peachtree and Marietta Streets,
the first draught of "The Ideal Nerve Tonic," concocted for use
by persons who couldn't continue to get French Wine Coca in a
dry county, was sold on Saturday, May 8, 1886. Not long afterward a customer somehow got his Coca-Cola in soda water
instead of the usual tap water. Mixed perhaps by accident, the

1899 staff, The Coca-Cola Company, 179 Edgewood Avenue; Asa G. Candler, front row center

bubbly stuff proved so refreshing that some persons began buying it for pleasure — not even seeking to relieve headache.

Once Asa Candler gained control of what had become a soda fountain beverage instead of a patent medicine, he dropped other products and took the plunge. Gambling at least $50,000 on the future of Coca-Cola, he incorporated the company in 1892 and had the trademark registered the following year.

Doc Pemberton's syrup was still being sold in bulk, mixed with

Early serving tray depicted then-idolized Hilda Clark

charged water at soda fountains — except in a Mississippi town where, unauthorized, a merchant began putting the bubbly stuff into stoppered bottles that could be reused.

Robert W. Woodruff

Initially indignant at this early form of business piracy, Candler decided to turn it into a plus for his company. He entered into a contract with two Chattanooga risk-takers, giving them what amounted to exclusive rights to bottle and then to sell Coca-Cola throughout the United States.

Charged enough to give it a great fizz and now available in take-home bottles as well as at soda fountains, Coca-Cola took off like a rocket — under Candler's astute and ever-growing advertising program. Calendars, serving trays, change trays, clocks, match books and dozens of other give-away items — often adorned with the faces of celebrities — boosted the Atlanta-born beverage to national and then to global prominence.

Coca-Cola made Asa G. Candler the first really wealthy man in Atlanta — and the first major philanthropist. After World War I, he sold out to a group headed by investment banker Ernest Woodruff for a paltry $25 million.

Four years later Woodruff's son Robert took over the company. During nearly sixty years in which he headed it, sales mounted steadily. Coca-Cola became the world's most familiar trademark. Entire bottling plants followed soldiers wherever they went during World War II; a company slogan proclaimed that "When you don't see a Coca-Cola sign, you have passed the borders of civilization."

Robert W. Woodruff's fortunes rose with those of his company. He gave away an estimated $250 million dollars — much of it so quietly that he became famous as "Mr. Anonymous." But philanthropy didn't bar him from a life of quiet affluence. His immense South Georgia quail plantation, at which he entertained presidents, was a hobby that even the Vanderbilts and Rockefellers couldn't have afforded earlier. Even his Christmas cards had a special touch of elegance — being prints of paintings executed for him by famous wildlife artist Athos Menaboni.

Soon after Woodruff's death not far short of the century mark, Coke celebrated its centennial year in 1986 — Atlanta's 149th. Partly perhaps out of natural exuberance at being one hundred years old and stronger than ever, the company made its biggest-ever acquisitions. It purchased Coke bottling operations of Beatrice Foods, Inc., rated at about seven percent of the U.S. can and bottle volume of the world's most widely used commercial product. For that small fraction of domestic bottling operations, the Atlanta-based company paid $1 billion. A few weeks later the company paid $1.4 billion for about thirteen percent more of U.S. bottling capacity. That purchase, from Chattanooga's pioneer bottlers, raised Coca-Cola's domestic share of the bottling operation to about thirty-one percent.

Meanwhile, Doc Pemberton's secret formula — bought by Candler for $2,300 — has withstood high-level legal challenges in order to remain one of the world's most coveted and most closely guarded commercial secrets.

Primeval Forest And Piggy-Back Hub

A first-time visitor to Atlanta wouldn't get the same tour that Margaret Mitchell gave to a New York editor in 1935. Two of the city's increasingly prominent sites combine the very old with the very new.

Fernbank Forest in DeKalb County, owned and guarded by the science center it nearly surrounds, is unique in the nation. Charles Russell, chairman of New York City's American Museum of Natural History, carefully examined it in 1949. He called it "an unduplicated jewel that gives metropolitan Atlanta a showpiece no other major city can match."

Some of the giant trees in the sixty-five-acre forest were standing when surveyors drove the stake marking the terminus of the W&A R.R. at a site about five miles away. According to Dr. Jim Skeen of Fernbank Science Center, such a forest requires 250 to 300 years for development.

In the Piedmont area, it usually begins with a heavy growth of pines. After 125 or so years, poplars and oaks begin to take over. At this point there is a big die-out of pines.

"Dead pines," says Skeen, "provide both nesting places and abundant food for many birds. One of them is the famous pileated woodpecker. Birds feed upon grubs. Grubs, in turn, multiply in dead pines." Now down to a minimum population of a few pairs, the spectacular pileateds have diminished because of a shortage of food — not because of guns. They're expected to return in droves in maybe fifteen or twenty years, when more dead pines will yield more grubs.

Guns of hunters — plus sketch pads of real estate developers — were kept out of Fernbank Forest largely through the influence of a five-foot woman. Strong-minded Emily Harrison was so determined to save the primeval tract as a teaching instrument for children that some who wanted to buy it called her a witch.

A few who knew her considered Miss Emily to be a bit fey, or daffy. Two or three of her relatives called her "crazy as a loon" when they learned she wouldn't even discuss selling to developers, at any price, the big tract of land left behind by her father.

Truly virgin, the forest that Miss Emily loved is the only one of its sort in the Piedmont Plateau that stretches from Alabama to New York. Even to the uninitiated, towering tulip poplars look their 250-plus years; so do many white oaks, hickories and northern red oaks.

Named for huge banks of native ferns plus other varieties transplanted by Emily Harrison, the forest has numerous nature trails — but when a tree falls and blocks a path, it lies where it fell. There has been as little human interference as possible.

From the forest-protecting woman plus joint heirs influenced by her, a non-profit corporation got one of the largest undivided pieces of real estate in the metro area for $35,000. For years the Harrison manor served as a museum; later the DeKalb County Board of Education got a long-term lease. Soon afterward, in 1967, a science center complete with an astronomical observatory and a planetarium was opened for use.

Nowhere in the nation is there a comparable science center operated by a public school system. Many Americans who never before had heard of it found themselves indebted to Fernbank on July 20, 1969.

Shortly after Neil Armstrong put his left foot upon the surface of the moon at 10:56 P.M. that day, a camera was lowered to the satellite's surface. Using the thirty-six-inch telescope at Fernbank, WSB-TV fed to networks of the world the first live pictures ever filmed on the moon.

Due to be completed in 1986, a $30 million museum of natural history will be unlike any in the Southeast. Architect Garland Reynolds, who prepared the site plan, was guided by Frederick L. Olmsted's work in Druid Hills. "Protection of the forest dictated the plan," he says. "Visitors to nearby Carter Center will not glimpse the museum unless they know about it and come looking for it."

Roughly three air miles away from the primeval forest, the Seaboard System Railroad is spending more than $20 million upon an intermodal facility that is expected to make Atlanta "piggyback hub of the region," if not of the nation.

Fernbank's telescope

Nat Welch, of the Georgia Freight Bureau, adopted the long-term goal of "piggyback center of the U.S.A." in 1983. To support it, he launched and now heads the International Intermodal Exposition — an annual world-class expo based, against all odds, in an inland city.

At Seaboard's Hulsey Yard, the new terminal is emerging as the most modern intermodal facility in the Southeast. An enormous crane transfers big cargo containers between truck trailers and rail flatcars. Many such cars go to nearby ports, where containers are transferred to deep-sea vessels. Freight moved in such fashion remains in a single huge package — or container — from point of production to point of use, which may be halfway around the world.

Founded as a railroad town, Atlanta — and the rest of the nation — gradually became dominated by other modes of transportation. Today's sixty-five-acre Hulsey Yard, almost precisely the size of Fernbank Forest, is within hearing distance of MARTA trains and traffic on interstate highways — to say nothing of landings and departures at Hartsfield International Airport.

Yet the rails are making a comeback, thanks to the piggyback concept which has spawned the fastest-growing segment of the railroad business. Mayor Andrew Young and the Georgia Freight Bureau announced a bold new goal: By 1990 they expect the city to be the piggyback center of the nation.

Pie in the sky? Perhaps not. Recent rail mergers have given Atlanta, for the first time, direct freight service to the Midwest, the Northeast and Canada. Nat Welch points out these mergers have already helped to propel the city from a regional role to national and international prominence in handling of heavy freight.

Almost within sight of trees that were already very old when the first W&A train puffed all the way from Atlanta to Marietta and back, the new piggyback hub promises to make old Junction City once more a key center of railroad progress.

Showcase Of Survival
In The City

Survival in spite of destruction was the theme of Margaret Mitchell's *Gone With the Wind* — destruction of railroads, bridges, plantation homes, slavery and the city of Atlanta — above all, the city. GWTW scholar Richard Harwell has underscored often-overlooked but persuasive evidence that for Peggy, Scarlett personified the city she so greatly loved and which, in her imagination, she saw go up in flames.

Survival in spite of construction is the theme of artist-architect-city builder John C. Portman's Peachtree Center. Construction of interstate highways, rapid transit systems, one-way streets and single-use high-rise buildings has left many humans feeling confined and trapped.

Mitchell's compelling theme, shaper of the novel that conveys it, insists that war and its aftermath make survival impossible for most — and difficult even for the very strong. Portman's architectural leitmotif declares that traditional construction of cities, according to long-accepted ideas, has made inner-city survival beyond accomplishment by many and incredibly hard even for the tough and resilient.

Margaret Mitchell put black marks upon white paper in order to produce an epic tale of the past. John Portman puts cement and steel and glass upon city blocks in order to produce an urban environment that affords sufficient space for good living — or the perception of such space, which may have the same subjective effect.

Though born in South Carolina, Portman was reared in Atlanta and earned a B.S. degree in architecture from Georgia Tech in 1950. He opened his own office three years later. Soon he found himself increasingly troubled by then-accepted developmental practices. It was taken for granted that final decisions concerning design would be made not by the architect but by developers who put up the money for a project.

John C. Portman

Balking at what nearly everyone else took for granted, Portman decided that he'd do more than design buildings. In order to have the creative input he wanted, he would finance, develop, design and control his own projects. What's more, he would do so from the viewpoint of the better-than-acceptable artist that he actually is.

Portman first put his revolutionary concepts into practice with Atlanta's Merchandise Mart, 240 Peachtree Street, in 1961. Six years later his second big project, the Regency Hyatt Hotel, created an international sensation.

Striding toward his goal of creating "pedestrian villages" in decaying inner cities, the man who habitually bills himself as architect/developer created a new and exciting design. He went in heavily for open space that was dominated by a twenty-two-story atrium, along with sculpture and fountains plus glass-enclosed elevators.

Design, he insisted, was based upon the human scale and human values in order to give persons who used the hotel a sense of being "both participants and observers." Just as some critics panned GWTW, a few architects have been scornful of Portman's end results. But Atlanta's Hyatt Regency made a quick and lasting impact upon hotel design, worldwide. Nearly every major

Atrium view of the world's tallest hotel

hotel built in the United States during the last twenty years bears the Portman imprint. Atlanta's Hyatt Regency remains vintage Portman — a classic as well as a prototype.

Completion of his seventy-three-story structure that is now the Westin Peachtree Plaza altered Atlanta's downtown profile and put the city into the record books again. At 731 feet from the Spring Street sidewalk to the roof, it became the tallest hotel in the world. Opening almost simultaneously with a new Hilton, it boosted Atlanta to third place in the nation as a convention center. Then the downtown hotel district expanded by the addition of Portman's Marriott Marquis — biggest hotel in the southeast.

Concurrently, Buckhead attracted so many builders that the once-suburban region soon will have more guest rooms than did pre-Portman downtown.

Had he stopped with hotels, the Atlanta architect/developer would be known and respected everywhere. But as his financial strength and his vision grew, Portman developed another radical new outlook. Instead of putting up single downtown buildings designed to meet narrow needs, he said, architects and developers should create "co-ordinated centers." In them, all human needs should be placed within walking distance. Provided with easy transitions between major spaces, such "people places" would serve as magnets drawing people to them willingly, not under compulsion.

That philosophy has produced Peachtree Center — world showcase of a vision that strives for survival in the inner city. Renaissance Center in Detroit, Embarcadero Center in San Francisco, and Marina Square in Singapore are likewise recognizable as Portman-produced in the genre of Atlanta's Peachtree Center.

First-time visitors to that prototype "people place" are impressed by glass elevators, awed by towering atriums, and delighted to find that they can easily move from building to building along aerial walkways. Michael Portman, who is director of corporate relations for the Portman Companies, says that his father's aerial bridges "are very carefully conceived in order to provide a strong connecting thread through the fabric of the city" in which linked structures form a self-contained chain of islands.

By 1986 buildings of Peachtree Center were linked by eleven walkways — with two more planned. One of them is, like the Westin Peachtree Plaza, a record-breaker. At 640 feet, it is one of the world's longest free-standing pedestrian pathways.

As the Portman Companies have expanded from architecture and engineering to real estate development, management, leasing, purchasing and consultation, they have made significant contributions to San Francisco, Los Angeles, New York, Chicago and numerous other cities. Worldwide, impact of the Atlanta architect/builder has been especially notable in Brussels, Singapore, Hong Kong, Jakarta, Shanghai and Kuala Lumpur.

In downtown Atlanta, the Portman vision does not have an end in sight. Developers are talking with enthusiasm of a return to inner-city living with initial housing for perhaps ten thousand persons who will live, work, eat, go to the theater and other places of entertainment . . . all vibrantly situated within the once-declining downtown.

In the second century of the growing metropolis that began as the terminus of a rail line linking the Chattahoochee and the Tennessee rivers, the best single spot from which to view the city

Atlanta, where the old and the new live in harmony

is the park built on land given by transplanted Yankee Lemuel P. Grant. There the skyline shaped by Peachtree Center is clearly visible — as a backdrop whose foreground is dominated by Civil War cannons that were fired until red-hot in the era when Atlanta was under the influence of another city-shaper named Sherman. In 1864, he rejoiced that his artillery and his torches had made it a place that couldn't possibly survive.

Today, we rejoice in his underestimation of a people and a city.

PHOTO AND ILLUSTRATION CREDITS

American Lung Association of Georgia, 77.

Atlanta Braves, 146.

Atlanta Chamber of Commerce, cover; 173.

Atlanta Cyclorama, 66; 70, top, middle, and bottom.

Atlanta Gas Light Co., 56.

Atlanta Historical Society, 4; 8; 9; 12, left and right; 13; 17; 26; 27, top; 29, top and bottom; 33, top and bottom; 36, bottom; 37; 42, bottom; 44; 45; 49, top; 63, 68; 70, top left; 74; 75; 108; 120; 123; 124; 149.

Atlanta Journal and *Atlanta Constitution,* 5; 39, top; 53; 59; 71; 79; 101; 104; 106; 109; 110; 115; 117, left; 122; 128, top; 134; 145; 150; 154.

Atlanta University, 65, top and bottom.

Atlanta World, 117, right.

Bankers First Corp., 10.

Battles & Leaders of the Civil War, 20, left and right; 36, middle.

The Coca-Cola Co., 90, top; 160; 161; 162; 163.

Delta Air Lines, 128, bottom; 129.

Emory University, 90, bottom; 93.

Fernbank Science Center, 167.

Fort McPherson, 83, bottom; 86; 87, left; 88, top and bottom.

Georgia Institute of Technology, 82; 83, top; 156.

Georgia-Pacific Corp., 130.

Georgia State Department of Archives and History, 3; 32, left; 36, top; 48; 49, bottom; 62; 100.

Georgia State University, 158.

Harper's Weekly, 9; 16, right.

The Herndon Home, 57.

Rawson Haverty, Sr., 58.

High Museum of Art, 152.

Wilbur G. Kurtz, Jr., 8; 13; 70, top right.

Library of Congress, 16, left; 23; 27, top; 29, bottom; 87, right.

Lockheed-Georgia, 131.

MARTA, 143, top, middle, bottom.

Macy's, 105.

Martin Luther King Center, 112.

National Archives, 22; 27, bottom; 29, top.

Portman Companies, 170; 171.

Rich's, 42, top.

Stone Mountain Park, 136, top and bottom; 139.

Tuskegee University, 60.

University of Georgia Libraries, 32, right; 138.

Wisconsin State Library, 69.

WSB-TV, 96; 97, top and bottom.

ACKNOWLEDGEMENTS

Editors and readers of the Sunday *Atlanta Journal-Constitution* rendered invaluable encouragement and assistance over a period of six years;

Wilbur G. Kurtz, Jr., made available the entire body of art produced by his father that depicts early Atlanta;

Franklin Garrett, of the Atlanta Historical Society, long ago issued a detailed account of Atlanta's development through the year 1939;

Edward M. Sears, editor of the *Palm Beach Post,* made available the photographic resources of the *Atlanta Journal* and the *Atlanta Constitution,* while managing editor of these newspapers.

In addition, the following institutions and individuals provided full and generous cooperation during every phase of research and writing: American Lung Association of Georgia; Atlanta Braves; Atlanta Chamber of Commerce; Atlanta Convention and Visitors Bureau; Atlanta Gas Light Company; Atlanta Historical Society; Atlanta Public Library; Atlanta University; *Atlanta World*; Coca-Cola Company; Delta Air Lines; Emory University; Fernbank Science Center; Fort McPherson; Georgia Department of Archives and History; Georgia Institute of Technology; Georgia-Pacific Company; Georgia State University; Rawson Haverty, Sr.; Herndon Home; High Museum of Art; Stanley Marcus of Neiman-Marcus, Dallas; Coretta Scott King; Martin Luther King Center; Oglethorpe University; Portman Companies; Garland Reynolds; Rich's; Seaboard System Railroad; Tuskegee University; and WSB-TV.

INDEX

Photos and illustrations indicated by italics